Introducing Microsoft® Silverlight® 1.0

Laurence Moroney

PUBLISHED BY
Microsoft Press
A Division of Microsoft Corporation
One Microsoft Way
Redmond, Washington 98052-6399

Library of Congress Control Number: 2007938162

Printed and bound in the United States of America.

1 2 3 4 5 6 7 8 9   QWT   2 1 0 9 8 7

Distributed in Canada by H.B. Fenn and Company Ltd.

A CIP catalogue record for this book is available from the British Library.

Microsoft Press books are available through booksellers and distributors worldwide. For further information about international editions, contact your local Microsoft Corporation office or contact Microsoft Press International directly at fax (425) 936-7329. Visit our Web site at www.microsoft.com/mspress. Send comments to mspinput@microsoft.com.

Microsoft, Microsoft Press, ActiveX, Expression, Expression Blend, Georgia, Internet Explorer, MSDN, Outlook, Silverlight, SQL Server, Verdana, Visual Studio, Windows, Windows Media, Windows NT, Windows Server, Windows Vista, and Wingdings are either registered trademarks or trademarks of Microsoft Corporation in the United States and/or other countries. Other product and company names mentioned herein may be the trademarks of their respective owners.

The example companies, organizations, products, domain names, e-mail addresses, logos, people, places, and events depicted herein are fictitious. No association with any real company, organization, product, domain name, e-mail address, logo, person, place, or event is intended or should be inferred.

This book expresses the author's views and opinions. The information contained in this book is provided without any express, statutory, or implied warranties. Neither the authors, Microsoft Corporation, nor its resellers, or distributors will be held liable for any damages caused or alleged to be caused either directly or indirectly by this book.

Acquisitions Editor: Ben Ryan
Developmental Editor: Devon Musgrave
Project Editor: Victoria Thulman
Editorial Production: Custom Editorial Productions, Inc.
Technical Reviewer: Kenn Scribner

Body Part No. X14-14867

I would like to dedicate this book to my wife, Rebecca,
who has been a constant companion and friend.
I am in awe of how blessed I am not just to know her,
but to be married to her. Thank you for making my life better.
Thank you also for being a great mother and friend
to our terrific children, Claudia and Christopher.

Contents at a Glance

Table of Contents

What do you think of this book? We want to hear from you!

Microsoft is interested in hearing your feedback so we can continually improve our books and learning resources for you. To participate in a brief online survey, please visit:

www.microsoft.com/learning/booksurvey/

Acknowledgments

I'd like to acknowledge a number of amazing people without whom this book would not be possible:

- Ben Ryan, who had faith in me as a writer in letting me write this very important book!
- Victoria Thulman, Content Project Manager, who was the person who pulled it all together!
- Kenn Scribner, an amazing technical reviewer, who kept me on my toes and who honed the piece of coal I produced into a diamond.
- Tim Sneath, manager of the Client Platform Evangelism team at Microsoft, and a constant friend and inspiration for this work.
- Ernie Booth, office mate, fellow Silverlight Evangelist, and deity of an undiscovered country.
- Karsten Januszewski, whose knowledge of XAML simply astounds me.
- Jaime Rodriguez, who I can only describe as a technology all-star!
- Ray Winninger, who I am sure will live long and prosper.
- Steve Cellini, who not only manages our entire department, but far more importantly, *inspires* us to great things.
- Mike Swanson, for giving me the thumbs-up despite my naïve answer to his interview question.
- Thomas Lewis, who knows how to rock.
- Steve Marx, whose Silverlight demos stretch my imagination.
- Barbara Lovelace, who drives me to understand design better than anyone.
- Joe Stegman, for driving a great product.
- Mike Harsh, whose terrific Silverlight blog keeps me on my toes!
- Others in the Silverlight and related teams whose valuable input, questions, feedback. and work made this product—and this book—possible: Adam Kinney, Arthur Yasinski, Barak Cohen, Brian Goldfarb, Catherine Heller, Cathy Guinan, Charles Finkelstein, Charles Torre, David Shadle, Duncan Mackenzie, Ed Maia, Eriko Asaoka, Eric Schmidt, Eric Lin, Erik Porter, Fumio Sekita, Good-Hyun Kim, Hai Yang Tang, Hong Chao Wang, James Clarke, Jason Suess, Jeannine Harsh, Jeff Sandquist, Jennifer Ritzinger, Jeremy Cath, Jeremy Mazner, Joshua Allen, Laura Foy, Leon Brown, Liwei Zhao, Mark Rideout, Mauricio Ordonez, Michael Lehman, Michael Suesserman, Peter Blois, Robert Hess, Ron Preston, Rory Blyth, Shirin Tabrizi, Ted Hu, Tim Aidlin, Vittorio Bertocci, and Yohei Takeuchi.

Introduction

Why Silverlight?

As the Web grows and evolves, so do the expectations of the Web user. When the first Web browser was developed, it was created to provide a relatively simple way to allow hyperlinking between documents. Then these early browsers were coupled with the cross-machine protocols encompassing the Internet, and suddenly documents stored on computer servers anywhere in the world could be hyperlinked to each other.

Over time, the people who were using the Internet changed—the user base expanded from a small group of people associated with universities and computational research to encompass the general population. And what had been an acceptable user interface for experts in the field was greatly lacking for commercial applications. People want high-quality user interfaces that are simple to use—and as more types of information, including many kinds of media files, are available on the Internet, it becomes more difficult to satisfy users' expectations about how easy it should be to access the information they want.

The need to supply users with sophisticated methods of accessing Internet resources that were easy to use led to advanced application technologies. One type of technology, for example, created "plug-in" browser tools that allowed the browser to use some of the user's local computational horsepower. ActiveX controls, Java Applets, and Flash applications are examples of plug-in technology. Asynchronous JavaScript and XML (AJAX) is another tool that has been introduced to develop new and exciting user interfaces that benefit from immediate partial updates. Using AJAX, the browser's screen area doesn't flash or lock up, since the need for full-page refreshes is reduced.

Although AJAX provides technology to enable developers to build Web sites that contain more complex content and are more dynamic than HTML alone could provide, AJAX does have its limitations. For example, it allows asynchronous communication with the server, which means that applications can update themselves using background threads, eliminating the screen flicker so often seen with complex Web user interfaces. But AJAX is strictly a browser-to-server communications mechanism. It lacks graphics, animation, video, and other capabilities that are necessary to provide for truly multimedia user interfaces.

Microsoft has built a Web user experience (UX) strategy to address these limitations by identifying three levels of desired user experience—"good," "great," and "ultimate," which are mapped to development and run-time technologies. These are combined in this book with a term you may find that I use a lot—"rich" or "richness." When I say "rich," I'm trying to describe a concept that's hard to put into words. It's the feeling you get when you use a traditional Web application, with the limitations built into the browser and HTML, versus a desktop application that has the entire operating system to call on for services and capability. The

Web applications of today just don't have the same feeling and capability as desktop applications, and the user generally realizes that they are limited by the technology. With Silverlight (and AJAX), the goal is to create Web applications that are much more like desktop applications, and ultimately, to create applications that are indistinguishable from desktop applications.

The lowest level of user experience, the "good" level, can be achieved with the browser enhanced by AJAX. This level identifies the baseline UX expectation moving forward from today—the type of asynchronous, dynamic, browser application empowered by AJAX.

The top or "ultimate" level is the rich client desktop, running Windows Vista and using the Windows Presentation Foundation (WPF) and the .NET Framework. These offer a run time that allows developers to create extremely rich applications that are easily deployed and maintained. Broadcast quality graphics, video, and animation are available at this level, as well as application services such as file-based persistence and integration with other desktop applications. In addition, WPF separates design and development technologies, so that user interfaces are designed and expressed in a new language called XML Application Markup Language (XAML). Design tools such as the Microsoft Expression series were aimed at designers who are now able to produce their work as XAML documents. Developers then use the resulting XAML to bring the designers' dreams to reality more easily by activating the XAML with code.

I mentioned that there are three levels in the UX strategy, because as AJAX and .NET/WPF evolved, it was obvious that there was room in the middle for a new technology that effectively takes the best of both worlds—the global scalability of the Internet application coupled with the richness of the desktop application. This level was named the "great" experience and represents the browser enhanced by AJAX with a new technology: Silverlight.

Silverlight is a plug-in for the browser that renders XAML and exposes a JavaScript programming interface. Thus, it allows designers and developers to collaborate when building Internet applications that provide the richness of desktop applications.

In this book, you'll be looking at Silverlight 1.0 and how to use it to enhance Web user experience. You'll also have a chance to take a look at Silverlight 1.1 and learn how this new version will allow you to further enhance your Web experience through the programming power of the .NET Framework.

Silverlight can change the way you think about building applications for the Web. Instead of Web sites, you will build Web *experiences*. At the heart of a great experience is great design, and with Silverlight, designers and developers can come together like never before, through XAML and the Microsoft Expression line of tools.

In this book, my goal is to help you understand the technologies that work together to develop and deploy a complete Silverlight Web application, from writing basic code that uses Silverlight to using advanced tools to create and deliver Silverlight content. When you have finished reading this book and have worked the examples, you should be ready to use what you've learned to enhance the Web applications you're developing *right now*. Imagine what you'll be able to do *tomorrow*!

Who This Book Is For

This book is written for developers who are already working every day to bring new and better Web applications to Internet users, and who are interested in adding this cutting-edge Microsoft technology to their store of knowledge—to find out how it can be applied as a tool to bring users more interesting, more capable, and more effective user interfaces. Development managers may also find the easy-to-read style useful for understanding how Silverlight fits into the bigger Microsoft Web technology picture, and with luck, will provide them with the technological background they need, so that when their developers come to them to talk about Silverlight—with excited looks on their faces—the manager will understand what the excitement is about!

What This Book Is About

In Chapter 1, "Introducing Silverlight," you'll get an introduction to Silverlight and take a quick tour of the features available in version 1.0. You'll also build some simple applications.

Chapter 2, "Silverlight and XAML," will introduce you to XAML and show you how you can use it to define your Web applications.

XAML and Silverlight offer APIs for managing timeline-based animation, which you will look into in some detail in Chapter 3, "XAML: Transformation and Animation." Expectations for the great user experience will involve using audiovisual media, and Chapter 4, "Silverlight and Media," offers an introduction to the media features available in Silverlight.

JavaScript is the programming heart of Silverlight 1.0, and you'll look into the JavaScript programming APIs in Chapter 5, "Programming Silverlight with JavaScript."

Silverlight supports Ink computing, which allows for new form factors when interfacing with the Web. You'll look into how Ink works with Silverlight in Chapter 6, "Using Silverlight with Ink."

Chapter 7, "Silverlight Server Programming," provides a look at how server applications can interact with and support Silverlight applications, and how Silverlight's open nature makes it ideal for cross-platform applications. You will see how to build server applications that deliver Silverlight content using Java, PHP, and ASP.NET.

Finally, in Chapter 8, "Silverlight Futures," you'll take a look into the future to find out how Silverlight is changing and growing. You'll see how the new "mini" .NET CLR will allow you to code high-performing applications for Silverlight, and how Silverlight can be extended with custom controls.

By the time you've finished reading this book, you will have a firm grip on what you need to build Silverlight applications. This book is designed to get you up and running quickly. I hope you'll have as much fun reading it as I did writing it!

Developing for Silverlight: System Requirements

Downloads for all the tools that you'll need to build Silverlight 1.0 and Silverlight 1.1. applications are listed here and are generally available at *http://silverlight.net/GetStarted/* (if they're not available at this site, you'll find links there to sites where they are available). The Silverlight Runtime for Windows is supported on Windows XP, Windows 2003, and Windows Vista using either the FireFox browser (1.5 and later) or Internet Explorer (6 and later). The Silverlight Runtime for Mac is supported on Mac OS 10.4.8 and later using either the FireFox browser (1.5 and later) or Safari.

To develop Silverlight applications as used in this book, you will need the following (again, available at *http://silverlight.net/GetStarted/*):

- Microsoft Visual Studio 2008
- Microsoft Expression Design
- Microsoft Expression Blend
- Microsoft Silverlight 1.0 Software Development Kit

Some of the book's samples will need the following tools:

- Microsoft ASP.NET Futures
- Microsoft Silverlight Tools for Visual Studio
- Microsoft Silverlight 1.1 Software Development Kit

The Companion Web Site

This book features a companion Web site that makes available to you all the code used in the book. This code is organized by chapter, and you can download it from the companion site at this address:

http://www.microsoft.com/mspress/companion/9780735625396

Support for This Book

Microsoft Press provides support for books and companion content at the following Web site:

http://www.microsoft.com/learning/support/books/

Questions and Comments

If you have comments, questions, or ideas regarding the book or the companion content, or questions that are not answered by visiting the sites just listed, please send them to Microsoft Press via e-mail to

mspinput@microsoft.com

Or via postal mail to

Microsoft Press

Attn: *Introducing Microsoft Silverlight 1.0* Editor

One Microsoft Way

Redmond, WA 98052-6399

Please note that Microsoft software product support is not offered through the above addresses.

Chapter 1
Introducing Silverlight

Silverlight represents the next step toward enriching the user's experience through the technology of the Web. The goal of Silverlight is to bring the same fidelity and quality found in the user interfaces associated with desktop applications to Web applications, allowing Web developers and designers to build applications for their clients' specific needs. It is designed to bridge the technology gap between designers and developers by giving them a common format in which to work. This format will be rendered by the browser without compilation and will be based on XML, making it easy to template and to automatically generate. The format is XAML–XML Application Markup Language.

Before XAML, a Web experience designer would use one set of tools to express a design using familiar technology. The developer would then take what the designer provided and would interpret it using the technology of his or her choice. The design would not necessarily transfer properly and problem-free into development, and the developer would need to make many alterations that could compromise the design. With Silverlight, the designer can use tools that express a design as XAML, and the developer can pick up this XAML, activate it with code, and deploy it.

Microsoft Silverlight is a cross-browser, cross-platform plug-in that was developed to deliver rich media experience and rich interactive Internet applications via the Web. It offers a full programming model that supports AJAX, .NET, and dynamic languages such as Python and Ruby. Silverlight 1.0 is programmable by way of actual Web technologies including AJAX, JavaScript and DHTML, and Silverlight 1.1 adds dynamic and .NET language support. This book will concentrate on version 1.0, but Chapter 8, "Silverlight Futures," does provide a peek into the future of Silverlight, including how to program it using C#, Ruby, and Python.

Silverlight and User Experience

Silverlight is designed to be part of a much larger ecosystem that is used to deliver the best possible end-user experience. There are a number of typical scenarios for accessing information via the Internet:

- Mobile devices
- Digital home products
- Unenhanced browser (no plug-ins)

- Enhanced browser (using plug-ins such as Flash, Java, or Silverlight)
- Desktop applications
- Office productivity software

Over the years, users' expectations about how these applications should work have evolved. For example, the *expectation* is that the experience of using an application on a desktop computer should provide more to the user than the same type of application on a mobile device, because, as users, we are accustomed to having much more power on the desktop than we do on a mobile device. In addition, many users assume that "because this application is on the Web," it may not have the same capacity level as a similar desktop application. For example, a user may have lower expectations about a Web-based e-mail application because they don't believe it can offer the same e-mail capability that office productivity software such as Microsoft Outlook provides.

However, as these platforms are converging, the user's expectations are also increasing—and the term *rich* is now commonly used to describe an experience above the current baseline level of expectation. For example, the term "rich Internet application" was coined in response to the increased level of sophistication that Web users were seeing in applications powered by AJAX to provide a more dynamic experience in scenarios such as e-mail and mapping.

This evolution in expectations has led to customers who now demand ever richer experiences that not only meet the needs of the application in terms of functionality and effectiveness but also address the perception of satisfaction that the user has with a company's products and services. This can lead to a lasting relationship between the user and the company.

As a result, Microsoft has committed to the User Experience (UX) and is shipping the tools and technologies that you as a developer can use to implement rich UX applications. Additionally, they are designed to be coherent—that is, skills in developing UX-focused applications will transfer across the domains of desktop and Web application development. So, if you are building a rich desktop application but need a Web version, then you will have a lot of cross-pollination between the two. Similarly, if you are building a mobile application and need an Internet version, you won't need two sets of skills, two sets of tools, and two sets of developers.

Concentrating on the Web, Figure 1-1 shows the presentation and programming models that are available today. As you can see, the typical browser-based development technologies are CSS/DHTML in the presentation model and JavaScript/AJAX/ASP.NET in the development model. On the desktop, with the .NET Framework 3.x, XAML provides the presentation model, and the framework itself provides the development model. There is an overlap between these, and this is where the Silverlight-enhanced browser provides a "best of both worlds" approach.

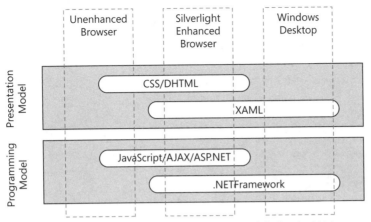

Figure 1-1   Programming and presentation models for the Web.

The typical rich interactive application is based on technologies that exist in the unenhanced browser category. The typical desktop application is at the other end of the spectrum, using unrelated technologies. The opportunity to bring these together into a rich application that is lightweight and runs in the browser is realized through the Silverlight-enhanced browser that provides the CSS/DHTML and XAML design model and the JavaScript/AJAX/.NET Framework programming model.

Silverlight achieves this by providing a browser plug-in that enhances the functionality of the browser with the typical technologies that provide rich user interfaces (UIs), such as timeline-based animation, vector graphics, and audiovisual media. These are enabled by the Silverlight browser-based XAML rendering engine. The rich UI may be designed as XAML, and because XAML is XML, and XML is just text, the application is firewall-compatible and (potentially) search-engine friendly. The browser receives the XAML and renders it.

When combined with technology such as AJAX and JavaScript, this can be a dynamic process—you can download snippets of XAML and graft them into your UI, or you can edit, re-arrange, or remove XAML that is currently in the render tree using simple JavaScript programming.

Silverlight Architecture

As I mentioned, the core functionality of Silverlight is provided by a browser plug-in that renders XAML and exposes its internal Document Object Model (DOM) and event programming model to the browser in a way that is scriptable via JavaScript.

The architecture that supports this is shown in Figure 1-2. The main programming interface that is exposed in Silverlight 1.0 is via the JavaScript DOM API. This allows you to catch user events that are raised within the application (such as mouse moves or clicks over a specific element) and have code to execute in response to them. You can call methods on the JavaScript DOM for XAML elements in order to manipulate them—allowing, for example, media playback to be controlled or animations to be triggered.

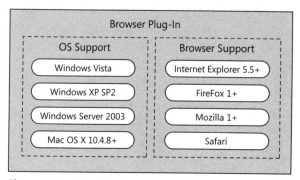

Figure 1-2   Silverlight architecture.

Additionally, the presentation run time ships with the software necessary to allow technologies such as WMV, WMA, and MP3 to be played back in the browser *without* any external dependencies. So, for example, Macintosh users do not need Windows Media Player to play back WMV content—Silverlight is enough. Underpinning the entire presentation run time is the presentation code, and this manages the overall rendering process. This is all built into the browser plug-in that is designed to support the major browsers available for both Windows and the Macintosh.

The architecture of a simple application running in the browser using Silverlight is shown in Figure 1-3.

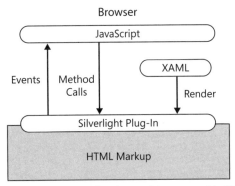

Figure 1-3   Application architecture with Silverlight.

As the application runs within the browser, it is typically made up of HTML markup. This markup contains the calls to instantiate the Silverlight plug-in. As users interact with the Silverlight application, they raise events that can be captured by functions written in JavaScript. In turn, program code written in JavaScript can make method calls against the elements within the Silverlight content to manipulate it, add new content, or remove existing content. Finally, XAML can be read by the plug-in and rendered. The XAML itself can exist inline in the page, externally as a static file, or as dynamic XAML returned from a server.

Your First Silverlight Application

What introduction would be complete without a "Hello World" application? In this section, you'll have the chance to look at all the pieces that make up a Silverlight application and how they work together. Although the application you build will be very simple, the principles of building a much more complex application are the same—and you'll be well on your way to understanding Silverlight development! You'll need no special tools—everything you do can be done with a simple text editor. You'll revisit these files again in Chapter 5, "Programming Silverlight with JavaScript."

Step 1: Silverlight.js

The first thing you'll need is the Silverlight.js file. This file contains everything you need to create a Silverlight component on your page. Silverlight is a browser plug-in that renders XAML and exposes a JavaScript programming interface. Browser plug-ins are implemented using special HTML tags called *object* and *embed*. Different browsers handle them differently, so instead of having to adjust them for a particular type of browser, it's a lot easier just to use the Silverlight.js file, which deals with the different browser implementations for you. It is available in the Silverlight Software Development Kit (SDK), which by default installs to \PROGRAM FILES\Microsoft Silverlight 1.0 SDK. You'll find Silverlight.js in the Resources directory. To use the file, simply include it with your Web project and provide a link on any page that will host the Silverlight control (you'll see this in Step 5 later in this section).

Step 2: XAML

A Silverlight user interface (UI) is defined using XAML—XML Application Markup Language. Some great resources to get you started with XAML can be found in the Silverlight Quick-Starts, task-based examples that provide tutorials to help you learn the features of Silverlight. The QuickStart tutorials are available at *http://www.silverlight.net/quickstarts*.

Our simple first application will use a XAML *Canvas* that contains a *TextBlock* control which, as its name suggests, renders text:

```
<Canvas
    xmlns="http://schemas.microsoft.com/client/2007"
    xmlns:x="http://schemas.microsoft.com/winfx/2006/xaml"
    Width="640" Height="480"
    Background="White"
    x:Name="Page">
    <TextBlock Width="195" Height="42" Canvas.Left="28" Canvas.Top="35"
        Text="Hello World!" TextWrapping="Wrap" x:Name="txt"/>
</Canvas>
```

This simple piece of XAML contains two components. The first component is the root *Canvas* element, which is present in every Silverlight XAML and defines the overall drawing surface. As you can see, we are using a 640 × 480 white *Canvas*. The second component is the *TextBlock* element I mentioned earlier. It renders the text "Hello World!" on the *Canvas*. This new XAML document should be saved and named. For this example, use the file name Page.xaml.

Keep in mind that XAML is just XML, so all of the conventions of XML apply. You can see that the *TextBlock* is a child node of the *Canvas*, and that XML attributes are used to define the properties of the objects. This allows for some cool scenarios, such as generating UI on demand from server applications using ASP.NET, Personal Home Page (PHP), or Java. We'll look at some of these possibilities later in this book.

Step 3: CreateSilverlight.js

It's good practice to host the code for creating the Silverlight component on your page in a separate JavaScript file. Although not essential, it is a useful step that promotes clean separation of code.

By convention, you would name this file CreateSilverlight.js, but of course you can name it anything you like as long as you reference it correctly when you assemble your HTML. Following is an example function that instantiates the Silverlight control in the browser:

```
function createSilverlight()
{
    Silverlight.createObjectEx({
        source: "Page.xaml",
        parentElement: document.getElementById("SilverlightControlHost"),
        id: "SilverlightControl",
        properties: {
```

```
            width: "100%",
            height: "100%",
            version: "1.0"
        },
        events: {
            onLoad: handleLoad
        }
    });
}
```

This function calls the *createObjectEx* function, which is implemented in Silverlight.js, an essential file that you added to your site in Step 1 of this example. You'll notice that an event handler, *handleLoad*, has been added to handle the *Load* event. You'll see how this is implemented in Step 4.

Step 4: Your Application Logic

This simple application allows you to click on the text block and cause the text to change from "Hello World!" to "You clicked me!" The code for this application is shown here:

```
var SilverlightControl;
var theTextBlock;
function handleLoad(control, userContext, rootElement)
{
    SilverlightControl = control;
    theTextBlock = SilverlightControl.content.findName("txt");
    theTextBlock.addEventListener("MouseLeftButtonDown", "txtClicked");
}
function txtClicked(sender, args)
{
    theTextBlock.Text = "You clicked me!";
}
```

The *handleLoad* method was defined as an event handler in the *createSilverlight* function. When Silverlight renders the control, it calls this method, passing it a reference to the control, the contents of the *userContext* variable (which can be set in the createSilverlight), and a reference to the root canvas element. You'll see all of this again in more detail in Chapter 5.

The *handleLoad* method locates the text block (named *txt*) and adds an event listener to its listener collection. The event that it is listening for is *MouseLeftButtonDown*, and when this event fires, the *txtClicked* function is invoked and the text is changed accordingly. This code should be saved to a new file named code.js and included in your project.

When you implement an event handler, as I have done with *handleLoad*, your function should accept parameters for *sender* (the originator of the event) and *args* (arguments associated with the event).

Step 5: Your HTML Page

Now it's time to put it all together with an HTML page that references each of the JavaScript files and embeds the Silverlight control. Following is the full HTML markup:

```
<!DOCTYPE HTML PUBLIC "-//W3C//DTD HTML 4.01 Transitional//EN"
  "http://www.w3c.org/TR/1999/REC-html401-19991224/loose.dtd">
    <html xmlns="http://www.w3.org/1999/xhtml">
    <head>
        <title>ZeroHero</title>
        <script type="text/javascript" src="Silverlight.js"></script>
        <script type="text/javascript" src="CreateSilverlight.js">
    </script>
        <script type="text/javascript" src="code.js">
    </script>
        <style type="text/css">
            .silverlightHost {
                height: 480px;
                width: 640px;
            }
        </style>
    </head>

    <body>
        <div id="SilverlightControlHost" class="silverlightHost">
            <script type="text/javascript">
                createSilverlight();
            </script>
        </div>
    </body>
    </html>
```

Upload all these files to your Web server and you're done.

This might have seemed to be a lot of work just to get a "Hello World" application working, but it also introduced you to the general principles involved with developing a Silverlight 1.0 application. You saw how to use Silverlight.js and CreateSilverlight.js, write XAML, load XAML into Silverlight, hook up events, and create run-time event handlers. The remainder of this book will examine those topics in more detail.

Silverlight and XAML

Now that we've taken a high-level look at the architecture of Silverlight and how a typical application will look, let's examine the base technology that holds the UX together: XAML.

XAML is an XML-based language that is used to define the visual assets of your application. This includes user interfaces, graphical assets, animations, media, controls, and more. It was introduced by Microsoft for the Windows Presentation Foundation (formerly Avalon), which is a desktop-oriented technology and part of the .NET Framework 3.0. It's designed, as discussed earlier, to bridge the gap between designers and developers when creating applications.

The XAML used in Silverlight 1.0 differs from that in the Windows Presentation Foundation in that it is a *subset* that is focused on Web-oriented features. So, if you're familiar with XAML from the Windows Presentation Foundation, you'll notice some missing tags and functionality, such as the <*Window*> element, data binding, and the rich control model.

XAML uses XML to define the UI using XML elements. At the root of every Silverlight XAML document is a *Canvas* element that defines the space on which your UI will be drawn. This root *Canvas* element contains the XML namespace declarations that Silverlight requires.

Here's an example:

```
<Canvas
  xmlns="http://schemas.microsoft.com/client/2007"
  xmlns:x="http://schemas.microsoft.com/winfx/2006/xaml"
  Width="640" Height="480"
  Background="White"
  >
</Canvas>
```

You will notice that two namespaces are declared. The typical XAML document contains a base set of elements and attributes as well as an extended set, which typically uses the *x:* prefix. An example of an extended namespace attribute is the commonly used *x:Name*, which is used to provide a name for a XAML element, allowing you to reference it in your JavaScript code. The root *Canvas* element declares the namespace location for each of these.

The *Canvas* element is a container. This means that it can contain other elements as children. These elements can themselves be containers for other elements, defining a user interface as an XML document tree. So, for example, the following is a simple XAML document containing a *Canvas* that contains a number of children, some of which are *Canvas* containers themselves:

```
<Canvas
  xmlns="http://schemas.microsoft.com/client/2007"
  xmlns:x="http://schemas.microsoft.com/winfx/2006/xaml"
  Width="640" Height="480"
  Background="Black"
  >
    <Rectangle Fill="#FFFFFFFF" Stroke="#FF000000"
        Width="136" Height="80"
        Canvas.Left="120" Canvas.Top="240"/>
    <Canvas>
        <Rectangle Fill="#FFFFFFFF" Stroke="#FF000000"
              Width="104" Height="96"
              Canvas.Left="400" Canvas.Top="320"/>
        <Canvas Width="320" Height="104"
              Canvas.Left="96" Canvas.Top="64">
          <Rectangle Fill="#FFFFFFFF" Stroke="#FF000000"
                    Width="120" Height="96"/>
          <Rectangle Fill="#FFFFFFFF" Stroke="#FF000000"
```

```
                        Width="168" Height="96"
                        Canvas.Left="152" Canvas.Top="8"/>
        </Canvas>
    </Canvas>
</Canvas>
```

Here you can see that the root canvas has two children, a *Rectangle* and another *Canvas*. This *Canvas* also contains a *Rectangle* and a *Canvas*, and this final canvas contains two more rectangles. This hierarchical structure allows for controls to be logically grouped together and to share common layout and other behaviors.

Silverlight XAML supports a number of shapes that can be combined together to form more complex objects. You'll find a lot more details about using XAML in Chapter 2, "Silverlight and XAML," but a few of the basic shapes available include the following:

- *Rectangle* Allows you to define a rectangular shape on the screen
- *Ellipse* Allows you to define an ellipse or circle
- *Line* Draws a line connecting two points
- *Polygon* Draws a many-sided shape
- *Polyline* Draws many line segments
- *Path* Allows you to create a nonlinear path (like a scribble)

In addition, XAML supports *brushes*, which define how an object is painted on the screen. The inside area of an object is painted using a *fill* brush, and the outline of an object is drawn using a *stroke*. Brushes come in many types, including solid color, gradient, image, and video.

Following is an example using a *SolidColorBrush* to fill an ellipse:

```
<Ellipse Canvas.Top="10" Canvas.Left="24"
         Width="200" Height="150">
    <Ellipse.Fill>
        <SolidColorBrush Color="Black" />
    </Ellipse.Fill>
</Ellipse>
```

In this case, the brush uses one of the 141 Silverlight-supported named colors or *Black*. You also can use standard hexadecimal RGB color notation for custom colors.

Fills and strokes also may have a gradient fill, using a gradient brush. The gradient is defined by using a number of *gradient stops* across a *normalized space*. So, for example if you want a linear gradient to move from right to left—phasing from black to white through shades of gray—you would define stops according to a normalized line. In this case, consider the beginning of the normalized line as the 0 point, and the end as the 1 point. So, a gradient from left to right in a one-dimensional space has a stop at 0 and another at 1. Should you want a gradient that transitions through more than two colors—from black to red to white, for example—you would define a third stop somewhere between 0 and 1. Keep in mind that when you create a fill, however, you are working in a two-dimensional space, so (0,0) represents the upper left-hand corner, and (1,1) represents the lower right-hand corner. Thus, to fill a rectangle with a gradient brush, you would use a *LinearGradientBrush* like this:

```
<Rectangle Width="200" Height="150" >
  <Rectangle.Fill>
    <LinearGradientBrush StartPoint="0,0" EndPoint="1,1">
      <LinearGradientBrush.GradientStops>
        <GradientStop Color="Red" Offset="0" />
        <GradientStop Color="Black" Offset="1" />
      </LinearGradientBrush.GradientStops>
    </LinearGradientBrush>
  </Rectangle.Fill>
</Rectangle>
```

XAML also supports text through the *TextBlock* element. Control over typical text properties such as content, font type, font size, wrapping, and more are available through attributes. Following is a simple example:

```
<TextBlock TextWrapping="Wrap" Width="100">
  Hello there, how are you?
</TextBlock>
```

Objects can be transformed in XAML using a number of transformations. Some of these include the following:

- ■ *RotationTransform*   Rotates the element through a defined number of degrees
- ■ *ScaleTransform*   Used to stretch or shrink an object
- ■ *SkewTransform*   Skews the object in a defined direction by a defined amount
- ■ *TranslateTransform*   Moves the object in a direction according to a defined vector
- ■ *MatrixTransform*   Used to create a mathematical transform that can combine all of the above

Transformations may be grouped so that you can provide a complex transformation by grouping existing ones. That is, you could move an object by translating it, change its size by scaling it, and rotate it simultaneously by grouping the individual transformations together. Here's a transformation example that rotates and scales the canvas:

```
<Canvas.RenderTransform>
   <TransformGroup>
      <RotateTransform Angle="-45" CenterX="50" CenterY="50"/>
      <ScaleTransform ScaleX="1.5" ScaleY="2" />
   </TransformGroup>
</Canvas.RenderTransform>
```

XAML supports animations through defining how their properties are changed over time using a timeline. These timelines are contained within a *storyboard*. Different types of animation include:

- *DoubleAnimation*   Allows numeric properties, such as those used to determine location, to be animated
- *ColorAnimation*   Allows colored properties, such as fills, to be transformed
- *PointAnimation*   Allows points that define a two-dimensional space to be animated

As you change properties, you can do it in a linear manner, so that the property is phased between values over a timeline, or in a "key frame" manner, in which you would define a number of milestones along which the animation occurs. We'll examine all of this in a lot more detail in Chapter 2.

Silverlight and the Expression Suite

Microsoft has introduced the Expression Suite of tools to provide a robust, modern set of tools for designers to express their work using artifacts that developers can include while developing using the Visual Studio tool suite.

There are four main tools in the Expression Suite:

- **Expression Web**   This is a Web design tool that allows you to use HTML, DHTML, CSS, and other Web standard technologies to design, build, and manage Web applications.
- **Expression Media**   This is a media asset management tool that permits you to catalog and organize these assets, including the facility to encode and change encoding between different formats.
- **Expression Design**   This is an illustration and graphic design tool that you can use to build graphical elements and assets for Web and desktop application user interfaces.
- **Expression Blend**   This tool is designed to let you build XAML-based user interfaces and applications for the desktop with WPF or for the Web with Silverlight.

In this chapter, we will take a look at Expression Design and Expression Blend and how they can used to build XAML for use in Silverlight.

Silverlight and Expression Design

Expression Design is a graphical design tool that allows you to build graphical assets for use in your applications. It's a huge and sophisticated tool, so this is just an overview of how it can be used for Silverlight XAML. Expression Design allows you to blend vector-based and raster-based (bitmap) images for complete flexibility.

It supports many graphical file formats for import, such as:

Windows Metafile and enhanced Metafile (.wmf, .emf)

- Photoshop (.psd)

- Graphical Interchange Format (.gif)

- PNG format (.png)

- Bitmaps (.bmp, .dib, .rle)

- JPEG formats (.jpeg, .jpg, .jpe, .jfif, .exif)

- Windows Media Photos (.wdp, .hdp)

- Tagged Image File Format (.tiff, .tif)

- Icons (.ico)

It supports export of the following image types:

- XAML

- Encapsulated Postscript (.eps)

- Adobe Illustrator (.ai)

- Portable Document Format (.pdf)

- Adobe Photoshop (.psd)

- Tagged Image File Format (.tif, .tiff)

- JPEG formats (.jpeg, .jpg)

- Windows Bitmap (.bmp)

- PNG format (.png)

- Graphical Interchange Format (.gif)

- Windows Media Photos (.wdp)

As you can see, Expression Design supports export of graphical assets as XAML files. Later in this chapter, you'll see how to use Expression Design to design the graphical elements of a simple media player, and you'll export these as XAML, which you can use in Expression Blend and Visual Studio to create an application.

Figure 1-4 shows the Export XAML dialog box in Expression Design. There are several format options, one of which is Silverlight (shown selected). This option will format your drawing using the subset of XAML elements that are usable by Silverlight, allowing you to import the resulting XAML into Visual Studio or Expression Blend to build your Silverlight application.

Figure 1-4   Exporting XAML from Expression Design.

Silverlight and Expression Blend

Expression Blend 2.0 has native support for the creation of Silverlight 1.0 and Silverlight 1.1 applications. When you launch Expression Blend and create a new project, you have three options for creating Silverlight projects, as you can see from Figure 1-5.

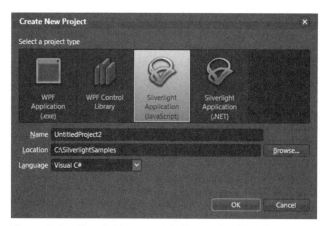

Figure 1-5   Silverlight support in Expression Blend.

The two options for Silverlight projects are:

- **Silverlight Application (JavaScript)**   This creates a Silverlight 1.0 project, giving you a folder that contains a simple Web application containing an HTML page that has the requisite scripts to embed a Silverlight object as well as a default XAML document containing a single canvas.

- **Silverlight Application (.NET) Application**   This creates a project for Silverlight 1.1. At present this is in prerelease, and this project template will give you the opportunity to try it out. There will be more on Silverlight 1.1 in Chapter 8.

This book will primarily cover Silverlight 1.0 JavaScript applications. Chapter 8, looking at the future of Silverlight, will discuss how the ASP.NET controls and .NET applications will be constructed using Silverlight.

Chapter 5 examines Silverlight 1.0 programming in JavaScript in more detail. We'll take a quick tour through a basic Silverlight 1.0 template application in the rest of this section, but more detail regarding this code and how to build your own is available in Chapter 5.

When you create a new Silverlight 1.0 Script application, your project will contain a default HTML file with an associated JavaScript file that is named Default.html.js. Expression Blend treats this as a "code-behind" JavaScript file in a manner that is similar to how Visual Studio treats the C# code-behind file associated with an ASPX page. Blend also creates a Scene.xaml file and a Scene.xaml.js file. Finally it gives you a copy of the Silverlight.js file that is part of the Silverlight SDK. This file manages the instantiation and downloading of the Silverlight plug-in for your users. You can see the project structure in Figure 1-6.

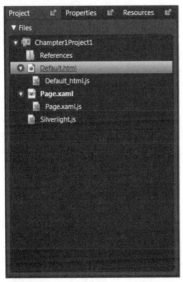

Figure 1-6   Project structure for Silverlight Script application.

The Default Web Page

Listing 1-1 shows the code for the basic Web page that is created for you by Blend for Silverlight projects.

Listing 1-1   Default.html from Silverlight Template

```
<!DOCTYPE HTML PUBLIC "-//W3C//DTD HTML 4.01 Transitional//EN"
"http://www.w3.org/TR/1999/REC-html401-19991224/loose.dtd">
<html xmlns="http://www.w3.org/1999/xhtml">
<head>
   <title>Chapter1Project1</title>

   <script type="text/javascript" src="Silverlight.js"></script>
   <script type="text/javascript" src="Default.html.js"></script>
   <script type="text/javascript" src="Page.xaml.js"></script>
   <style type="text/css">
     .silverlightHost {
       height: 480px;
         width: 640px;
       }
   </style>
</head>

<body>
   <div id="SilverlightControlHost" class="silverlightHost">
      <script type="text/javascript">
         createSilverlight();
      </script>
   </div>
</body>
</html>
```

As you can see, it imports three JavaScript files: Silverlight.js, Default.html.js, and Page.xaml.js. You'll be looking at each of these files later in this chapter.

The Silverlight control instantiation takes place in the <div> at the bottom of the page. This contains a call to a script called *createSilverlight*, which is implemented in Default.html.js. This is the typical programming pattern used for Silverlight applications—the instantiation of the control is contained in an external JavaScript script. This keeps your page code much cleaner.

Listing 1-2 contains the JavaScript code from Default.html.js.

Listing 1-2   Default.html.js Code-Behind

```
function createSilverlight()
{
   var scene = new Chapter1Project1.Page();
   Silverlight.createObjectEx({
      source: "Page.xaml",
      parentElement: document.getElementById("SilverlightControlHost"),
      id: "SilverlightControl",
      properties: {
         width: "100%",
         height: "100%",
         version: "1.0"
      },
      events: {
         onLoad: Silverlight.createDelegate(scene, scene.handleLoad)
      }
   });
}


if (!window.Silverlight)
   window.Silverlight = {};

Silverlight.createDelegate = function(instance, method) {
   return function() {
      return method.apply(instance, arguments);
   }
}
```

This code contains the createSilverlight function that you saw referred to in Default.html.. This can create a new Silverlight object using either the createObject or the createObjectEx function. When using the latter function, the syntax for specifying the parameters uses the JavaScript Object Notation (JSON) syntax as shown in this example.

The first parameter is the source XAML. This can be a reference to a static external file (which is used in this case as Page.xaml), a reference to the URL of a service that can generate XAML, or a reference to a named script block on the page that contains XAML.

The second parameter is the parent element. This is the name of the DIV that contains the Silverlight control. As you can see in Listing 1-1 this is called *SilverlightControlHost*.

The third parameter is the ID that you want to use for this control. If you have multiple Silverlight controls on a page, you need to have a different ID for each.

The fourth parameter is the property settings for the control properties. These can include simple properties such as width, height, and background color as well as complex ones. More complex property settings include:

- ■ *inplaceInstallPrompt*   Determines the install type for Silverlight. If this is set to *true*, the user implicitly accepts the license and directly downloads and installs the plug-in. If it is set to *false*, the user is directed to *www.silverlight.net*, and from that site, can accept the license and download the plug-in.

- ■ *isWindowless*   If set to *true*, the control is considered *windowless*, meaning that you can overlay non-Silverlight content on top of it.

- ■ *framerate*   Determines the maximum frame rate that for animations.

- ■ *version*   Determines the minimum Silverlight version your application will accept.

The fifth parameter is used to map events to event handlers. The events are implemented in a JavaScript class called *Scene*, which was declared at the top of the function:

```
var scene = new Chapter1Project1.Page();
```

The *createSilverlight* function declares that the *onLoad* event should be handled by a member function of the scene class called *scene.handleLoad*. It does this by creating a delegate using this syntax:

```
onLoad: Silverlight.createDelegate(scene, scene.handleLoad)
```

This class is implemented in the JavaScript code-behind for Page.xaml called Page.xaml.js. You can see this in Listing 1-3.

Listing 1-3   JavaScript Code-Behind Page.xaml

```
if (!window.Chapter1Project1)
    window.Chapter1Project1 = {};

Chapter1Project1.Page = function()
{
}

Chapter1Project1.Page.prototype =
{
    handleLoad: function(control, userContext, rootElement)
    {
        this.control = control;

        // Sample event hookup:
        rootElement.addEventListener("MouseLeftButtonDown",
            Silverlight.createDelegate(this, this.handleMouseDown));
    },

    // Sample event handler
    handleMouseDown: function(sender, eventArgs)
    {
        // The following line of code shows how to find an element by name and
        // calls a method.
        // this.control.content.findName("Timeline1").Begin();
    }
}
```

Here you can see JavaScript code to create a class called *Chapter1Project1.Page*. It contains two member functions, *handleLoad* and *handleMouseDown*.

The function *handleLoad* adds another event listener for the *MouseLeftButtonDown* event by creating a delegate associating this event and the *handleMouseDown* function, which is also defined within this JavaScript script.

Thus, the template application creates a default HTML file that contains an instance of Silverlight with a single canvas that fires an event when it loads. The load event wires up the mouse down event, demonstrating that event declaration, delegation, and handling are available at both design time and run time.

In the next section, you'll build out a simple media player application that puts this theory into action. More detail on how to use JavaScript to program Silverlight applications is available in Chapter 5.

Building a Silverlight Media Player

It's always best to put the theory into practice with some hands-on experience, so for the rest of this chapter, you'll see how to use what you've learned to create a full Silverlight application.

You'll use all of the tools that we've discussed so far. It's not *necessary* to do this—you could do everything with Visual Studio or Expression Blend—but it's useful to demonstrate the tools continuum and how the tools are optimized for the workflow of building an application for the User Experience.

You'll build out a simple video player, using graphical assets designed with Expression Design. As Expression Design is capable of using raster and vector graphics, you'll create the look and feel of the video player in Expression Design, and then Export this as XAML. You'll then take the XAML and load it into Blend, where you will add the video control and wire it up to a video file. You'll also implement the code that handles the play, stop, and pause controls.

Designing the Assets in Expression Design

To get started, let's create a new graphic in Expression Design by selecting New from the File menu. This opens a dialog box that you can use to create a new image and specify its dimensions and resolution. Figure 1-7 shows an example of a 500 × 500 pixel design to which a bitmap of the Silverlight logo has been added.

Figure 1-7   Starting to design the video player in Expression Design.

The next thing to do is to add some vector graphic assets to represent the controls for the video playback. On the left side of the screen, you'll see the controls toolbar, and on this there is a list of available shapes. Hold the mouse down on the rectangular shape, and you'll get a pop-up palette of available shapes, as shown in Figure 1-8.

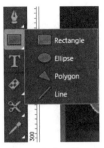

Figure 1-8   Shapes tools palette in Expression Design.

From the palette, choose Ellipse and draw a circle on the design surface. For this example, draw a small circle under the Silverlight image on the bitmap. You'll see the red outline of a circle drawn on the surface of the graphic. See Figure 1-9 for an example.

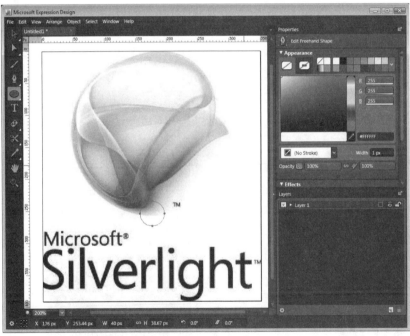

Figure 1-9   Adding a vector ellipse.

Move over to the Appearance dialog box and select the stroke and fill that you want to use. Figure 1-10 shows the Appearance dialog box with a gradient fill and a white stroke selected for the circle.

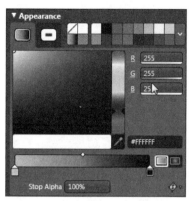

Figure 1-10   Editing the Appearance properties.

If you select similar options, you will see a gradient-filled circle surrounded by a white border. Use the Copy and Paste commands to make two more instances of the circle and put them on either side of the first. Your screen should now look something like Figure 1-11.

Figure 1-11   Three copies of the filled ellipse.

Now use the polygon tool to draw a triangle within the center circle and then use the rectangle tool to draw a square within the circle on the left and two tall rectangles within the circle on the right to create the traditional Play, Stop, and Pause icons, respectively. Figure 1-12 shows the completed icons.

Figure 1-12   Adding the Stop, Play, and Pause buttons.

You're now ready to export your creation as XAML and use it within Expression Blend to implement the application. To do this, select File Export and then select the name that you want to use for the file. The Export dialog box (Figure 1-13) will appear. Make sure that you select Silverlight as the export type.

Figure 1-13 Exporting the Video Player application.

Click Export to create the XAML. In addition, a subdirectory will be created with a copy of the .png file in it. In the next section, you'll use this XAML within a new Expression Blend project.

Implementing the Application in Expression Blend

Microsoft Expression Blend allows you to create a Silverlight 1.0 application, as you learned earlier in the chapter. Launch Blend and select New Silverlight 1.0 Script Application from the File/New menu options.

This will create a new Expression Blend project containing the files described earlier in this chapter. You can add the XAML by right-clicking on the project in the project Explorer window and then selecting Add New Item. You'll see the three control icons, but not the background graphic, as this was exported into a subdirectory of the directory where you saved the XAML file. Repeat the process to add a new item and browse to the graphic.

You'll notice if you look at the XAML view that the picture is implemented using the *Image* element. This has a *Source* attribute that contains the subdirectory the image that you created using Design. Since you have imported the image to your Blend project, it's now in the same directory as the XAML, and thus cannot be found. So, edit the *Source* element to remove the subdirectory and set the source attribute to the name of the image (i.e., Source="image0.png"). Now you'll see the image in Blend.

Adding Video Using the Media Element

Silverlight provides audio and visual media using the *MediaElement* control. This isn't present on the toolbar by default. You can add this by clicking the New Tools icon at the bottom of the toolbar to open the Assets Library dialog box, shown in Figure 1-14.

Figure 1-14   Adding a new control using the Asset Library.

You can search the Asset Library using the text box at the upper left-hand corner of the dialog box. Type **Media** (as shown in Figure 1-14), and you'll see the *MediaElement* listed on the System Controls list. Select it and then double-click it to add it to the toolbar.

Next, add the media element to the scene by selecting its tool on the toolbar and dragging out the shape that you want it to cover. You'll see a grey rectangle with a camera icon in the center as a placeholder for the media. See Figure 1-15.

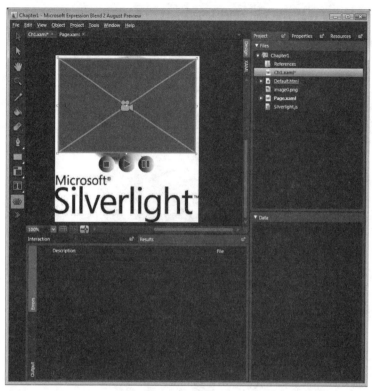

Figure 1-15 Adding a new *MediaElement* to your design.

On the right-hand side of the screen, you can see the Properties dialog box that provides options you can use to configure this video element, as shown in Figure 1-16.

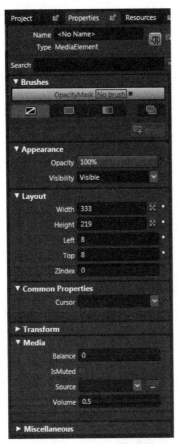

Figure 1-16   The *MediaElement* Properties dialog box.

You can search the properties using the search box near the top of the dialog box. This is useful for complex objects that have a lot of properties associated with them. To set the video source, use the *Source* property and an available WMV file. The file will be added to the project, and the XAML will be updated to configure the media element to indicate the path to the video in its source attribute. In the XAML editor, set the *MediaElement*'s name to "vid". Your XAML will now look like this:

```
<MediaElement Width="408" Height="232" Canvas.Left="48" Canvas.Top="40" Source="Test.wmv"
x:Name="vid"/>
```

If you test the application now by pressing F5, you'll see the Silverlight content rendered in the browser and the video will play back. The next thing to do is to configure the buttons to catch events and to control the media element in response to them.

Wiring the Video Controls

You're now going to wire events to the controls, but since each control is made up of a number of elements (the background circle and the foreground icon), you can group them into a single canvas and then wire the elements to the canvas together to make things easier.

To do this, make sure that the direct selection tool (it looks like a white arrow) is selected on the toolbar, and then hold the Ctrl key as you select the background circle and the foreground icon of the video control. So, for example, for the Stop control icon, select the background circle and the foreground rectangle.

Once you've selected the elements, open the Object menu, then select Group Into, and then select Canvas. This will group the controls into a *Canvas* container. See Figure 1-17.

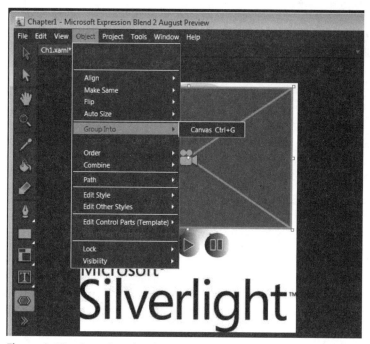

Figure 1-17   Grouping the elements into a *Canvas* container.

The Objects and Timeline dialog box shows the controls in your scene, and you'll now see three new *Canvas* elements that can be opened up to see the contained *Ellipse*, *Rectangle*, and *Path* elements.

It's a good idea, for programmability, to name these *Canvas* elements. Double-click *Canvas* in the Objects and Timeline dialog box and it will be highlighted in yellow. Then you can edit its name using the Properties dialog box.

See Figure 1-18 for an example that shows one *Canvas* element that has been named *btnPlay*, and another *Canvas* element has been selected to edit.

Figure 1-18   Editing the *Canvas* elements.

If you switch to the XAML view, you'll see the *Canvas* elements listed. Following is an example of the XAML for the Play button, which was named *btnPlay*:

```
<Canvas x:Name="btnPlay" Width="52.667" Height="52.667"
        Canvas.Left="236.111" Canvas.Top="390.333">
<Ellipse x:Name="Ellipse" Width="52.6667" Height="52.6667"
      Stretch="Fill" StrokeThickness="2"
      StrokeLineJoin="Round" Stroke="#FFFFFFFF">
   <Ellipse.Fill>
      <LinearGradientBrush StartPoint="0.0189873,0.5" EndPoint="0.981013,0.5">
         <GradientStop Color="#FFE3D2E3" Offset="0"/>
         <GradientStop Color="#FF000000" Offset="1"/>
      </LinearGradientBrush>
   </Ellipse.Fill>
  </Ellipse>
<Path x:Name="Path" Width="22.3439" Height="25.6458"
      Stretch="Fill" StrokeLineJoin="Round" Stroke="#FFFFFF00"
      Data="F1 M 274.867,415.771L 253.524,403.448L 253.524,428.094L
            274.867,415.771 Z "
      Canvas.Left="16.913" Canvas.Top="12.615">
   <Path.Fill>
      <LinearGradientBrush StartPoint="-0.0223775,0.500001"
                           EndPoint="1.02238,0.500001">
         <GradientStop Color="#FFAE69AE" Offset="0"/>
         <GradientStop Color="#FF000000" Offset="1"/>
      </LinearGradientBrush>
   </Path.Fill>
  </Path>
</Canvas>
```

You can see that the *Canvas* element envelopes the *Ellipse* and *Path* elements (the *Path* element implements the triangle shape), so if you define an event handler for the *Canvas* element, it will apply to all of the children of that component, too. So, for example, you can trap the user pressing the mouse button on an element using the *MouseLeftButtonDown* event. If you define this for the *Canvas*, then clicking on the ellipse or on the triangle will raise that event.

Now let's add the event handling for the Play button. On the *Canvas* that represents the Play button, you can add an attribute called *MouseLeftButtonDown*, which contains the name of the desired JavaScript function to execute when the user clicks it. Here's the XAML code with the new attribute highlighted:

```
<Canvas x:Name="btnPlay" Width="52.667" Height="52.667" Canvas.Left="236.111"
Canvas.Top="390.333" MouseLeftButtonDown="handlePlay">
```

Now, all you need to do is create the *handlePlay* function. Open the Default.html.js file and add the following code at the bottom of the existing code:

```
function handlePlay(sender, eventArgs)
{
    sender.findName("vid").play();
}
```

The *findName* function is exposed by the Silverlight DOM API, and it allows you to search for a named element and create a reference to it. In this case, it finds the element called *vid*, which is the *MediaElement* you placed and named earlier. It then calls the *play* method on this to play the video. You can follow a similar approach to wire the *pause* and *stop* methods to their respective *Canvas* elements and write JavaScript that calls the *pause* and *stop* methods, also exposed by the *MediaElement*.

To run and test the application, make sure that the *createSilverlight* function (in Default.html.js) uses the XAML file as its source. If your XAML was called vplayer.xaml, your *createSilverlight* function will look like this:

```
function createSilverlight()
{
    var scene = new Chapter1Project.Scene();
    Sys.Silverlight.createObjectEx({
        source: "Page.xaml",
        parentElement: document.getElementById("SilverlightControlHost"),
        id: "SilverlightControl",
        properties: {
            width: "100%",
            height: "100%",
            version: "1.0"
            },
        events: {
            onLoad:Silverlight.createDelegate(scene, scene.handleLoad)
        }
    });
}
```

Now you can run the application and control the video playback using the three video controls.

This simple demonstration is intended to show the workflow between Expression Design and Expression Blend, and how they can be used to put together a simple video player application.

It's hard-coded for a single video, and typically, the next step would be to add some new functionality, perhaps to select videos from a list or to give a common dialog box that allowed users to find a video—let your imagination guide you. As you work with Silverlight, ASP.NET, and AJAX, you will see how these technologies all neatly fit together to allow you to build your application the way that you want it, in an easy and productive manner. It should be a fun ride!

Summary

In this chapter, you were introduced to Silverlight and how it fits into the overall Web and user-experience landscape. You discovered how technology from Microsoft is applied to current UX scenarios and were introduced to an overview of the Silverlight architecture.

Additionally, you saw how the Microsoft Expression Suite is designed to complement traditional development tools such as Visual Studio for creating Silverlight applications. You specifically learned how Expression Design is used to build graphical assets and how Expression Blend is used to link these together into an interactive application.

You took a brief tour of XAML to discover how it is used to implement rich user interfaces, before diving in with both feet and building a simple video player. By the end of this chapter, you should have a better understanding of what it takes to design, implement, and code a user interface in Silverlight 1.0 using JavaScript. Now it's time to go deeper. In the next few chapters, you'll learn more about the Silverlight API, starting with a more detailed examination of Silverlight XAML in the next chapter.

Chapter 2
Silverlight and XAML

XAML is at the core of your Silverlight application. You use it to define your graphical assets, your interactions, your animations, and your timelines. It's based on XML, so everything is defined in text markup using attributes to declare properties, methods, and events.

In this chapter, we'll look at the common XAML components used to define the visual elements of your application. First we'll examine how to make a layout, including how elements can be drawn on the screen relative to their containers and each other. We'll also look at the various brushes that can be used to fill shapes and controls, as well as the strokes that can be used to draw their outlines. Then you will learn about paths and geometries, how they can help you generate complex shapes and groups of shapes, and how you can use them to clip other objects or fills. Finally, we'll look at the controls that use these XAML components, including the *Canvas* that is at the heart of Silverlight layout, and we'll examine how to render text using the *Glyphs* and *TextBlock* controls.

XAML Layout Properties

Briefly, you use the *Canvas.Left* and *Canvas.Top* properties to lay out controls in XAML. These properties are referred to as *attached* properties, which simply means that they are available globally in your XAML code, or they modify a property that's really exhibited by their parent. In addition to this, the *Canvas.ZIndex* attached property may be used to determine the Z-order position of the item, which defines the topmost object to be rendered if two or more overlap. The default Z-order behavior in XAML is that the last item drawn (farthest down in the XAML document) is topmost, but this can be overridden using *Canvas.ZIndex*.

So, consider the following XAML. It shows the code for a *Canvas* containing two rectangles. These use *Canvas.Left* and *Canvas.Top* to determine their upper-left corners relative to the canvas that contains them.

```
<Canvas>
    <Rectangle Fill="Red" Width="200" Height="128"
               Canvas.Left="8" Canvas.Top="8"/>
    <Rectangle Fill="Black" Width="280" Height="80"
               Canvas.Left="40" Canvas.Top="32"/>
</Canvas>
```

The black rectangle is drawn on top of the red one, as shown in Figure 2-1.

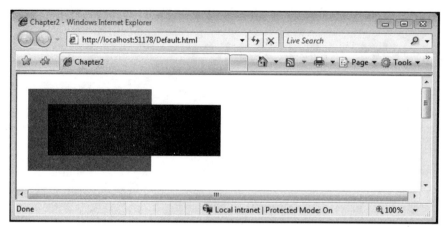

Figure 2-1 Rectangle layouts.

The red rectangle is positioned 8 pixels from the left and 8 pixels from the top of the parent canvas. The black one is positioned 40 pixels from the left and 32 pixels from the top. The black rectangle appears on top because it was the last one rendered.

You can use *ZIndex* to override this behavior. You can specify *ZIndex* to be a numeric value, and the highest numbered *ZIndex* will appear on top of lower numbered ones, as you see in the following code:

```
<Canvas>
    <Rectangle Canvas.ZIndex="2"
               Fill="Red" Width="200" Height="128"
               Canvas.Left="8" Canvas.Top="8"/>
    <Rectangle Canvas.ZIndex="1"
               Fill="Black" Width="280" Height="80"
               Canvas.Left="40" Canvas.Top="32"/>
</Canvas>
```

As shown in Figure 2-2, the red rectangle now appears on top of the black one, as you would expect, because the *ZIndex* value for the red rectangle is higher than the *ZIndex* value for the black rectangle.

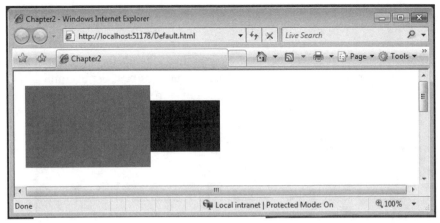

Figure 2-2   Changing the Z-order of elements.

XAML Brushes

You use *brushes* in XAML to determine how shapes are drawn and filled. In the earlier example, you saw that the two rectangles were filled using the known colors *Red* and *Black,* respectively. These are simple examples of using brushes. The next sections describe the more complex set of *Brush* types that XAML supports.

SolidColorBrush

The *SolidColorBrush* fills an area with a solid color. The color can be a named value, such as *Red* or *Black*, or it can be described in hexadecimal values indicating the alpha, red, green, and blue channel intensities. For example, the color white is described as *#FFFFFFFF* in hexadecimal notation, and the color red would be *#FFFF0000*.

LinearGradientBrush

The *LinearGradientBrush* fills an area with a linear gradient defined in two-dimensional space. The default gradient is defined using a normalized rectangle—a rectangle with its upper-left corner at (0,0) and its lower-right corner at (1,1). This defines the gradient as extending from the upper-left corner to the lower-right corner. If you define a color at each of these points, Silverlight will draw the gradient between them.

As an example, consider the following rectangle definition:

```
<Canvas>
   <Rectangle Width="200" Height="128" Canvas.Left="8" Canvas.Top="8">
      <Rectangle.Fill>
         <LinearGradientBrush>
            <GradientStop Color="#FF000000" Offset="0"/>
            <GradientStop Color="#FFFFFFFF" Offset="1"/>
         </LinearGradientBrush>
```

```
        </Rectangle.Fill>
      </Rectangle>
</Canvas>
```

This XAML snippet defines a *LinearGradientBrush* that extends from the upper-left corner to the lower-right corner of the rectangle. The first gradient stop, at the beginning of the gradient, is black (#FF000000), and the second gradient stop, at the end of the gradient, is white (#FFFFFFFF). You can see this rectangle rendered in Figure 2-3.

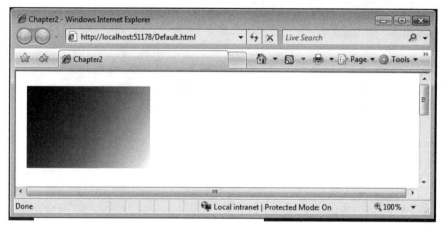

Figure 2-3   Using the *LinearGradientBrush*.

Changing the Gradient Direction

You can change the direction of the brush by setting the *StartPoint* and *EndPoint* properties of the *LinearGradientBrush*. To change the gradient fill direction to lower left to upper right, you can set these to (1,0) and (0,1) respectively, as shown:

```
<Rectangle Width="200" Height="128" Canvas.Left="8" Canvas.Top="8">
    <Rectangle.Fill>
      <LinearGradientBrush StartPoint="0,1" EndPoint="1,0">
        <GradientStop Color="#FF000000" Offset="0"/>
        <GradientStop Color="#FFFFFFFF" Offset="1"/>
      </LinearGradientBrush>
    </Rectangle.Fill>
</Rectangle>
```

Figure 2-4 shows how this rectangle is rendered.

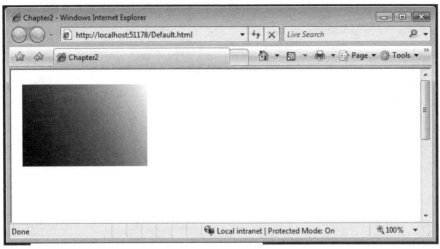

Figure 2-4 Changing the gradient direction.

Adding Gradient Stops

The previous examples show the minimum number of gradient stops, which is two. You can create other gradient stops containing colors and locations to control the gradient. For example, if you want your gradient to range from black to white to black again, you can define three stops like this:

```
<Rectangle Width="200" Height="128" Canvas.Left="8" Canvas.Top="8">
    <Rectangle.Fill>
        <LinearGradientBrush>
            <GradientStop Color="#FF000000" Offset="0"/>
            <GradientStop Color="#FFFFFFFF" Offset="0.5"/>
            <GradientStop Color="#FF000000" Offset="1"/>
        </LinearGradientBrush>
    </Rectangle.Fill>
</Rectangle>
```

The first stop, at position 0, is black; the second, half way along the gradient at position 0.5, is white; and the third stop, at the end of the gradient at position 1, is black again. If you render this, you will see something like the rectangle shown in Figure 2-5.

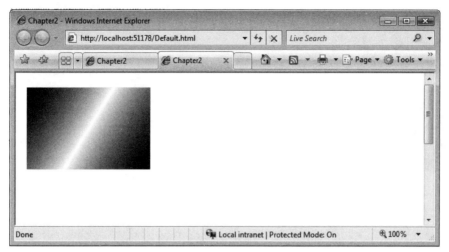

Figure 2-5   Using gradient stops.

The gradient stops are positioned using the *Offset* parameter, so, to move the white section of this gradient closer to the upper-left corner, you simply change its *Offset* so that it is closer to zero, as shown in this XAML snippet:

```
<Rectangle Width="200" Height="128" Canvas.Left="8" Canvas.Top="8">
    <Rectangle.Fill>
        <LinearGradientBrush>
            <GradientStop Color="#FF000000" Offset="0"/>
            <GradientStop Color="#FFFFFFFF" Offset="0.1"/>
            <GradientStop Color="#FF000000" Offset="1"/>
        </LinearGradientBrush>
    </Rectangle.Fill>
</Rectangle>
```

You can see this how this changes the appearance of the rendered rectangle in Figure 2-6.

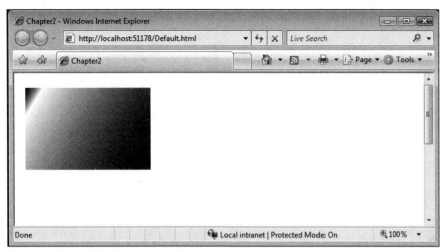

Figure 2-6   Positioning the gradient stop.

You can achieve some nice effects by experimenting with how you position and direct gradients. These properties can be used to fill shapes or to define strokes, as you will see later in this chapter.

RadialGradientBrush

The *RadialGradientBrush* is similar to the *LinearGradientBrush* from a definition point of view, but it defines a circular gradient, with 0 marking the center of the circle of the gradient and 1 marking its outer edge. It's easier to show this by example, so consider this XAML:

```
<Rectangle Width="200" Height="128" Canvas.Left="8" Canvas.Top="8">
   <Rectangle.Fill>
      <RadialGradientBrush>
         <GradientStop Color="#FF000000" Offset="0"/>
         <GradientStop Color="#FFFFFFFF" Offset="1"/>
      </RadialGradientBrush>
   </Rectangle.Fill>
</Rectangle>
```

This fills the rectangle with a gradient brush with black at its center and white at its outer edge, as shown in Figure 2-7. Notice that since the outer edge of the rectangle is white, you see an ellipse. This is because the background color of the rectangle is the same as the outer gradient stop color for the brush.

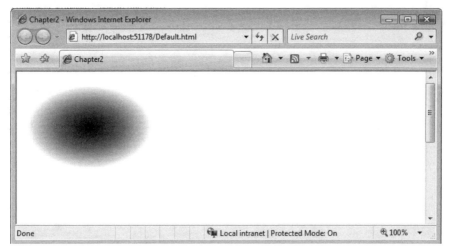

Figure 2-7   Filling a rectangle with the *RadialGradientBrush*.

Gradient stops for the *RadialGradientBrush* are defined using similar methods to those used for gradient stops for the *LinearGradientBrush*.

Setting the Focal Point

When you apply a fill with the *RadialGradientBrush*, you can set the focal point for the radial by using the *GradientOrigin* property. You use this to set the point from which the gradient emanates, normally at the center of the circle. Despite the circular nature of the *RadialGradientBrush*, the focal point is set in a rectangular normalized space. So, if you want the focal point to be at the upper-left corner, set the *GradientOrigin* to (0,0); if you want it at the lower-right corner, set the *GradientOrigin* to (1,1). The following example shows the gradient with the focal point set toward the lower right of the object, at (0.7,0.7):

```
<Rectangle Width="200" Height="128" Canvas.Left="8" Canvas.Top="8">
   <Rectangle.Fill>
      <RadialGradientBrush GradientOrigin="0.7, 0.7">
         <GradientStop Color="#FF000000" Offset="0"/>
         <GradientStop Color="#FFFFFFFF" Offset="1"/>
      </RadialGradientBrush>
   </Rectangle.Fill>
</Rectangle>
```

Figure 2-8 shows how it is rendered.

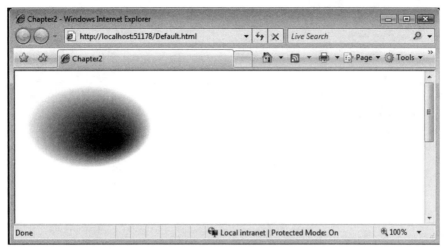

Figure 2-8   Setting the focal point of a *RadialGradientBrush*.

Changing the *SpreadMethod*

You can use the *SpreadMethod* property to determine how the gradient repeats. There are three possible values for *SpreadMethod*: *Pad*, *Reflect*, and *Repeat*. *Pad* fills the circle with the gradient as specified and is the default value. Figures 2-7 and 2-8 show a basic *RadialGradient-Brush* with a spread set to *Pad*.

Following is the XAML for a rectangle filled with a gradient brush with its *SpreadMethod* set to *Reflect*. You can see the results in Figure 2-9.

```
<Rectangle Width="200" Height="128" Canvas.Left="8" Canvas.Top="8">
   <Rectangle.Fill>
      <RadialGradientBrush SpreadMethod="Reflect">
         <GradientStop Color="#FF000000" Offset="0"/>
         <GradientStop Color="#FFFFFFFF" Offset="1"/>
      </RadialGradientBrush>
   </Rectangle.Fill>
</Rectangle>
```

This causes the gradient to reflect, as you can see in Figure 2-9. The gradient is defined to range from black to white, but then starts phasing from white to black again as a reflection.

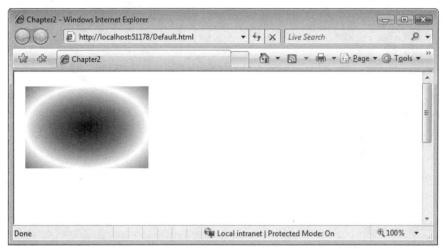

Figure 2-9   Using the *Reflect SpreadMethod*.

Similarly, you can use the *Repeat* method to repeat the gradient from black to white. Figure 2-10 shows the result of this. Where the gradient would normally stop, the gradient pattern is instead repeated, repeating the phasing from black to white to the outside edges of the rectangle.

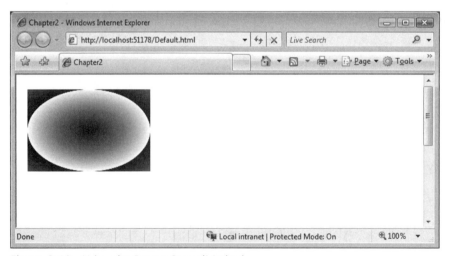

Figure 2-10   Using the *Repeat SpreadMethod*.

Setting the Radius of the *RadialGradientBrush*

You use the *RadiusX* and *RadiusY* properties to specify the desired radius for the gradient. The default value for each is 0.5. If you specify a value less than this, you will paint more than one circle with the *SpreadMethod* defining the rendering behavior. If you specify a value greater than 0.5, you effectively "zoom" the gradient.

For example, following is a XAML snippet that defines a *RadialGradientBrush* with *RadiusX* and *RadiusY* set to 0.1 and *SpreadMethod* not set (so it defaults to *Pad*).

```
<Rectangle Width="200" Height="128" Canvas.Left="8" Canvas.Top="8">
   <Rectangle.Fill>
      <RadialGradientBrush RadiusX="0.1" RadiusY="0.1">
         <GradientStop Color="#FF000000" Offset="0"/>
         <GradientStop Color="#FFFFFFFF" Offset="1"/>
      </RadialGradientBrush>
   </Rectangle.Fill>
</Rectangle>
```

This renders the rectangle with a *RadialGradientBrush* using a 0.1 radius, so it is effectively one-fifth the size of the objects we saw earlier. You can see this in Figure 2-11.

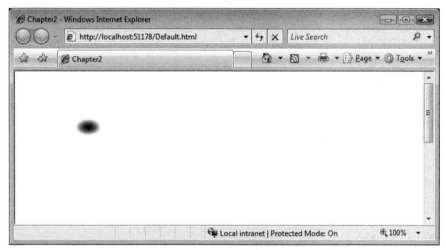

Figure 2-11   Setting the radius of the *RadialGradientBrush*.

When combined with the *SpreadMethod*, you can get some interesting effects. You can see an example with a *SpreadMethod* set to *Reflect* in Figure 2-12.

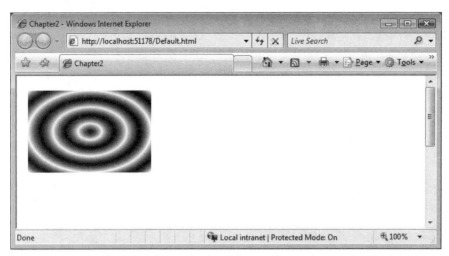

Figure 2-12 Combining a change in the radius setting and *SpreadMethod*.

Using *ImageBrush*

To fill a space with an image, you use the XAML *ImageBrush*. The default behavior will stretch the brush to fit the image to maintain the image's aspect ratio. The following XAML fills the contents of a rectangle with an *ImageBrush*:

```
<Rectangle Width="200" Height="128" Canvas.Left="8" Canvas.Top="8">
   <Rectangle.Fill>
      <ImageBrush ImageSource="smily.jpg" />
   </Rectangle.Fill>
</Rectangle>
```

You can see the results of this in Figure 2-13.

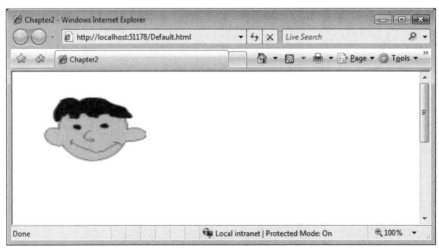

Figure 2-13 Filling the rectangle with the *ImageBrush*.

Stretching the Image

You can specify how the image fills the area that it is painting with the *Stretch* property. You can specify this using one of several different stretch modes: *None*, *Uniform*, *UniformToFill*, and *Fill*.

None renders the image untouched—no stretching takes place. *Uniform* scales the image to fit the rectangle dimensions but leaves the aspect ratio untouched. *UniformToFill* scales the image to completely fill the output area but preserves its aspect ratio (clipping the image as necessary). *Fill* will scale the image to fit the output dimensions using independent scaling on the x- and y-axes. This will distort the image to completely fill the available space.

You can see these options in action in Figure 2-14, which shows four rectangles that have been filled with the same image, but using the different stretch modes.

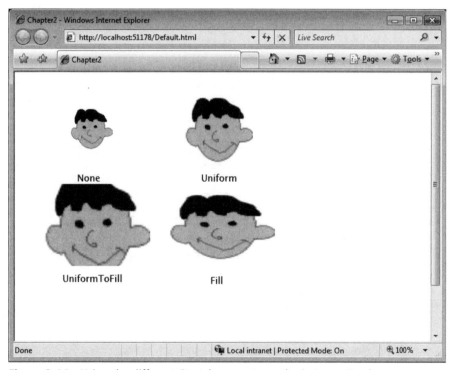

Figure 2-14   Using the different *Stretch* property modes in *ImageBrush*.

Aligning the Image

The alignment of the image along the x- and y-axes can be set with the *AlignmentX* and *AlignmentY* properties. You can align the image to the left, right, or center on the x-axis, and to the top, center, or bottom on the y-axis. Note that if you are stretching the image to fill the surface, then setting the alignment will have no effect—it will only work when *Stretch* is set to *None*. Following is an example of aligning the image to the right and bottom:

```
<Rectangle Stroke="Black" Width="200" Height="128" x:Name="r1">
   <Rectangle.Fill>
      <ImageBrush ImageSource="smily.jpg" Stretch="None"
                  AlignmentX="Right" AlignmentY="Bottom" />
   </Rectangle.Fill>
</Rectangle>
```

You can see how it will appear in Figure 2-15.

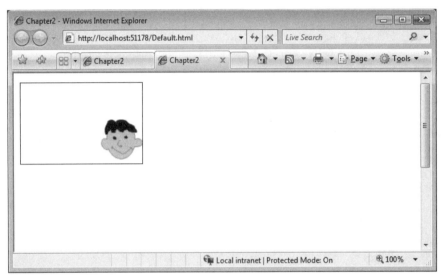

Figure 2-15   Using image alignment.

VideoBrush

The *VideoBrush* allows you to fill an area with video. I'll discuss this brush in more detail in Chapter 4, "Silverlight and Media," where I also describe the *MediaElement* control more completely.

XAML Visual Properties

Beyond brushes and canvas settings, there are a number of other properties provided by XAML to help you to control the appearance of your object. These allow you to set an object's dimensions, opacity, cursor behavior, and stroke.

Using XAML Dimension and Position Properties

XAML dimensions are set using the *Height* and *Width* properties, each of which takes a *double* value. To create a rectangle that is 100 pixels wide and 200 pixels high, for example, you would define your XAML as follows:

```
<Rectangle Fill="Black" Width="100" Height="200" />
```

In addition, keep in mind that the *Top* and *Left* properties attached to the parent *Canvas* are used to specify the relative position of the object.

Consider the following XAML:

```
<Canvas>
  <Canvas Canvas.Top="40" Canvas.Left="40">
    <Rectangle Canvas.Top="40" Fill="Black" Width="100" Height="200" />
  </Canvas>
</Canvas>
```

Assume the outmost *Canvas* is the root canvas for the page. The *Rectangle* will be drawn 80 pixels down from the top of the page as a result. Its parent *Canvas* is 40 pixels down, and the *Rectangle* is 40 pixels down from its parent, for a total of 80 pixels.

Using Opacity

There are two ways that you can set the opacity of an object. The first is to use the alpha channel in the brush that is used to fill the object. The following XAML will create a black rectangle on top of an image:

```
<Image Source="smily.jpg" />
<Rectangle Fill="#FF000000" Width="100" Height="200" />
```

The *Fill* is set to black (because the red, green, and blue channels are all set to zero), and the alpha is set to opaque (filled with #FF). You can make the rectangle semitransparent by changing the alpha channel value:

```
<Image Source="smily.jpg" />
<Rectangle Fill="#77000000" Width="100" Height="200" />
```

You'll see that the rectangle now appears grey, and the image is visible underneath it.

The second method is to use the *Opacity* property, which takes a value from 0 (totally transparent) through 1 (totally opaque). This property is used in conjunction with the alpha channel in the brush. If you use the brush color #77000000 to fill the shape, for example, and then set *Opacity* to 1, the rectangle will still be somewhat opaque. If you set it to 0, the rectangle will be totally transparent.

Using the *Opacity* property is useful when it comes to animating the *Opacity* of an object. It makes it easy to fade an object in or out using a *DoubleAnimation*. You can learn more about animation in Chapter 3, "XAML: Transformation and Animation."

Cursor Behavior

Most XAML elements allow you to specify how the mouse will appear when it hovers over it using the *Cursor* property. The *Cursor* property is set to a value from the *MouseCursor* enumeration:

- **Arrow**   Displays the typical default arrow cursor
- **Default**   No cursor preference; use the parent's cursor if it is specified
- **Hand**   Displays a pointing hand cursor, usually used for a link
- **IBeam**   Specifies an I-beam cursor; typically used for text selection
- **None**   No cursor
- **Wait**   Specifies an hourglass indicating a busy wait state

Controlling *Stroke*

The *Stroke* property is used to determine how a shape's outline is painted on the screen. This is different from how it is *filled* with a brush. In a rectangle, for example, the stroke determines how the outline of the rectangle is drawn.

The *Stroke* is set by using a *Brush*. Following is an example of XAML that renders a rectangle using a simple stroke to specify a black outline:

```
<Rectangle Stroke="Black" Canvas.Left="40" Canvas.Top="40" Width="100" Height="200">
```

The *Stroke* property is in fact using a *Black SolidColorBrush* in this case. It is syntactically equivalent to the following XAML:

```
<Rectangle Canvas.Left="40" Canvas.Top="40" Width="100" Height="200">
   <Rectangle.Stroke>
      <SolidColorBrush Color="Black" />
   </Rectangle.Stroke>
</Rectangle>
```

Using this syntax (defining the brush as an attached stroke property), it is possible to specify different types of brushes to draw the shape's stroke. Following is an example of using a *LinearGradientBrush* to paint the rectangle's stroke:

```
<Rectangle StrokeThickness="10" Canvas.Left="40"
           Canvas.Top="40" Width="100" Height="200">
   <Rectangle.Stroke>
     <LinearGradientBrush >
        <GradientStop Color="#FF000000" Offset="0"/>
        <GradientStop Color="#FFFFFFFF" Offset="0.5"/>
        <GradientStop Color="#FF000000" Offset="1"/>
        </LinearGradientBrush>
```

```
    </Rectangle.Stroke>
</Rectangle>
```

You can see how this appears on the screen in Figure 2-16.

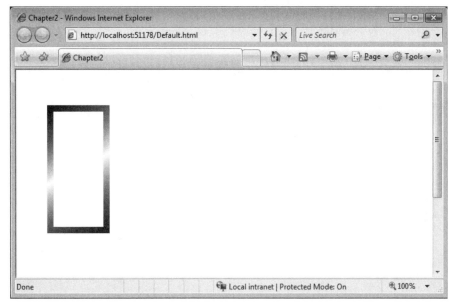

Figure 2-16   Using a *LinearGradientBrush* to define a shape's stroke.

Setting Stroke Width

You may have noticed in this example that the width of the stroke was set to 10. This was done to better demonstrate the gradient, which doesn't show up well using the default stroke width value of 1.

The stroke width is set using the *StrokeWidth* property. This specifies the stroke width in pixels:

```
<Rectangle StrokeThickness="10" Stroke="Black" Canvas.Left="40" Canvas.Top="40" Width="100"
Height="200" />
```

Setting Stroke Dash

The *StrokeDashArray* property is used to set the stroke dash pattern. This is combined with the *StrokeDashCap* and *StrokeDashOffset* properties to allow stroke dash fine tuning.

To set the stroke of the rectangle to be dashed with a repeating pattern of dashes, you define an array of *double* values that represent the length of the dashes as well as the space between them. To define a dash pattern using a dash 4 units long, followed by a space 1 unit long, followed by a dash 2 units long, followed by a space 1 unit long before repeating, you would set the *StrokeDashArray* property to (4,1,2,1). Here's an example:

```
<Rectangle StrokeThickness="10" Stroke="Black" Canvas.Left="40" Canvas.Top="40" Width="100"
Height="200" StrokeDashArray="4,1,2,1"/>
```

Figure 2-17 shows how this is drawn on the screen.

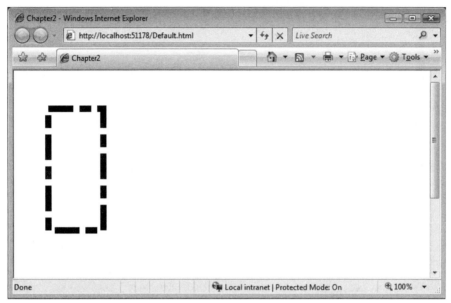

Figure 2-17   Setting the dash pattern for the stroke using *StrokeDashArray*.

You can see that these dashes are rectangular in shape, with squared dash edges. You can change this using the *StrokeDashCap* property. This property is set to a value from the *PenlineCap* enumeration. It can contain the following values:

- **Flat**   This is the default value, and it specifies that the cap doesn't extend beyond the end of the line—it is the same as not having a cap.

- **Round**   This specifies a semicircle with the same diameter as the line thickness.

- **Square**   This specifies a square end cap.

- **Triangle**   This specifies an isosceles triangle end cap, with the base length equal to the thickness of the stroke.

Following is an example of using the *StrokeDashCap* to set a rounded dash cap:

```
<Rectangle StrokeThickness="10" Stroke="Black" Canvas.Left="40" Canvas.Top="40" Width="100"
Height="200" StrokeDashArray="4,1,2,1" StrokeDashCap="Round"/>
```

Figure 2-18 shows how this will appear on the screen.

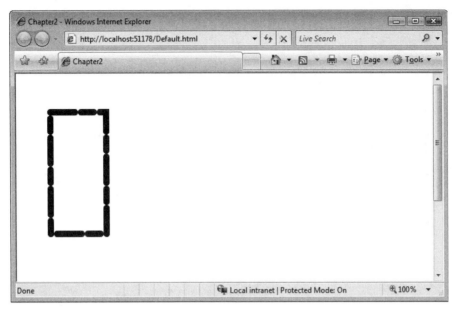

Figure 2-18   Using the *StrokeDashCap* property.

Controlling Line Joins

If you look at the previous examples, you will notice that the dash lines intersect at the corners and are drawn squared off. This is considered a line join, and the *StrokeLineJoin* property allows you to control how the pen behaves at this line join. This property is set to the *PenLine-Join* enumeration, which can contain three values:

- **Bevel**   Shave off the edges of the join.
- **Miter**   Keep the sharp edges.
- **Round**   Round the edges of the join.

This XAML creates a rectangle with the line join type set to *Bevel*:

```
<Rectangle StrokeThickness="10" Stroke="Black" Canvas.Left="40" Canvas.Top="40" Width="100"
Height="200" StrokeLineJoin="Bevel" />
```

You can see how this is drawn in Figure 2-19.

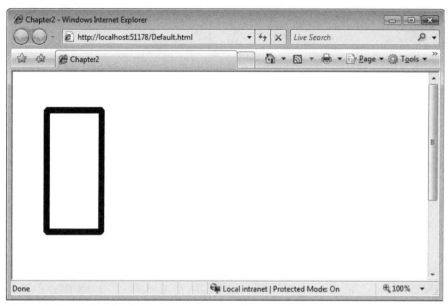

Figure 2-19   Using the *StrokeLineJoin* to specify a beveled corner.

Shapes in XAML

XAML Supports a number of basic shapes that can be used to create more complex objects. These shapes are:

- **Ellipse**   Draws an ellipse—a circle is an ellipse with equal radius distances for *X* and *Y*
- **Rectangle**   Draws a rectangle—a square is a rectangle with equal distances for *X* and *Y*
- **Line**   Draws a line
- **Path**   Draws a series of connected lines and curves according to a path language
- **Polygon**   A closed shape made up of a connected series of lines
- **Polyline**   A series of connected straight lines

We'll look at how to create each of these shapes in the following subsections.

Using the *Ellipse* Object

The *Ellipse* shape is used to draw an ellipse or circle. You control the *Ellipse* by setting its height property to the desired vertical diameter (i.e., twice the desired vertical radius) and its width property to the desired horizontal diameter. If these values are equal in value, the XAML will render a circle. The *Ellipse* outline is drawn using a *Stroke*, and the *Ellipse* is filled using a *Brush*.

Using the *Rectangle* Object

The *Rectangle* shape is used to draw a rectangle or square. You control the size of the shape using the *Width* and *Height* properties. If these properties are equal, you end up with a square. Like the *Ellipse*, the outline of the *Rectangle* is drawn using a *Stroke*, and it is filled using a *Brush*.

You can round the corners of a *Rectangle* shape using the *RadiusX* and *RadiusY* properties. You set these to a *double* specifying the radius of the desired circle. They default to 0.0, indicating no rounding. As the *RadiusX* and *RadiusY* are set independently, you can obtain elliptical rounding effects by using different values.

Following is an example of a rectangle with rounded corners. *RadiusY* is set to 40, and *RadiusX* is set to 20, indicating that the corners will be smoother vertically than they are horizontally:

```
<Rectangle Fill="Black" Canvas.Left="40" Canvas.Top="40"
        Width="100" Height="200" RadiusX="20" RadiusY="40" />
```

You can see the results of these settings in action in Figure 2-20.

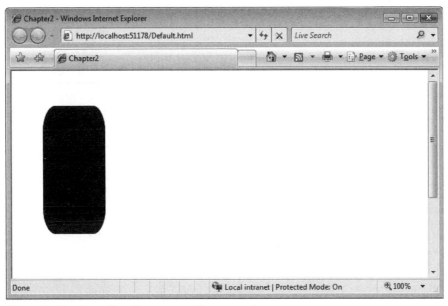

Figure 2-20   Rounding the corners of a rectangle.

Using the *Line* Object

You can draw a simple line in XAML using the *Line* object. This allows you to specify its (X1,Y1) and (X2,Y2) coordinates with the line to be drawn between them. These coordinates are relative to the upper-left position of the line, specified using *Canvas.Top* and *Canvas.Left* in the usual manner. Note that you need to specify the line stroke using at least a stroke color before the stroke will be drawn.

Consider the following XAML:

```
<Line X1="40" Y1="40" X2="100" Y2="100" Stroke="Black" />
```

This will draw a line from (40,40) to (100,100). However, if you add *Canvas.Top* and/or *Canvas.Left*, then the line will be drawn relative to that. So, the following XAML will draw the line from (40,140) to (100,200), assuming there is no positioning on the parent canvas. If there is, Silverlight will draw the line relative to the parent positioning.

```
<Line Canvas.Top="100" X1="40" Y1="40" X2="100" Y2="100" Stroke="Black" />
```

Using Paths and Geometries

The *Path* object draws a connected series of lines and curves. These lines and curves can be defined using a geometry.

The *EllipseGeometry* defines the path as a simple ellipse. Here's an example:

```
<Path Stroke="Black">
  <Path.Data>
    <EllipseGeometry RadiusX="100" RadiusY="100" />
  </Path.Data>
</Path>
```

The *EllipseGeometry* uses *RadiusX* and *RadiusY* to specify the dimensions of the ellipse that makes up the geometry. It also allows you to define the center point of the ellipse using the *Center* attribute. Following is an example:

```
<Path Stroke="Black">
   <Path.Data>
     <EllipseGeometry RadiusX="100" RadiusY="100" Center="50,50" />
   </Path.Data>
</Path>
```

The *LineGeometry* defines the path as a single line, starting at the *StartPoint* and ending at the *EndPoint*. These are set simply using string x- and y-coordinates, so the upper-left corner is specified as (0,0). Here's an example of a *LineGeometry*:

```
<Path Stroke="Black">
  <Path.Data>
    <LineGeometry StartPoint="10,10" EndPoint="100,100" />
  </Path.Data>
</Path>
```

The *RectangleGeometry* defines the path as a single rectangle, using the *Rect* property to define the dimensions of the rectangle. This is a string of four values, corresponding to the top, left, height, and width of the rectangle. So, to draw a rectangle that is 100 by 200 pixels, with its upper-left corner at (0,0) ,you would use the following *Path*:

```
<Path Stroke="Black">
  <Path.Data>
    <RectangleGeometry Rect="0,0,100,200" />
  </Path.Data>
</Path>
```

The *PathGeometry* is used to put together a complex path of different segments, including arcs, Bezier curves, lines, poly-Bezier curves, polyquadratic Beziers curves, and quadratic Bezier curves. Segments can be collected into a *PathFigure*, and one or more *PathFigure* objects make up a *PathGeometry*. The *PathGeometry* also sets the starting point of the path. If you have multiple segments, the starting point for each segment will be the last point of the previous segment.

The *ArcSegment* Object

The *ArcSegment* object draws a simple elliptical arc between two points. You have a number of different properties to set to define the arc:

- **Point**   Sets the starting point for the arc
- **Size**   Sets the x and y radius of the arc
- **RotationAngle**   Sets the rotation angle—that is, how far the angle is rotated around the x-axis
- **IsLargeArc**   Sets the "largeness" of the arc, where an arc over 180 degrees is considered large
- **SweepDirection**   Sets the drawing direction of the arc (*Clockwise* or *CounterClockwise*)

Here's an example of a *Path* with a single arc segment, with these properties demonstrated:

```
<Path Stroke="Black">
  <Path.Data>
    <PathGeometry>
      <PathFigure>
        <ArcSegment Point="100,100" Size="200,200"
          RotationAngle="10" IsLargeArc="False"
          SweepDirection="ClockWise" />
      </PathFigure>
    </PathGeometry>
  </Path.Data>
</Path>
```

The *LineSegment* Object

You can add a line to a *PathSegment* using the *LineSegment* object. This simply draws a line from the current or starting point to the point defined using its *Point* property. So, to draw a line from (100,100) to (200,200) and then another back to (200,0), you create a *PathFigure* containing multiple line segments like this:

```
<Path Stroke="Black">
    <Path.Data>
        <PathGeometry>
            <PathFigure StartPoint="100,100">
                <LineSegment Point="200,200" />
                <LineSegment Point="200,0" />
            </PathFigure>
        </PathGeometry>
    </Path.Data>
</Path>
```

The *PolyLineSegment* Object

As its name suggests, the *PolyLineSegment* allows a number of lines to be drawn simply by providing the points. The first line is drawn from the start point to the first defined point, the second line from this point to the second defined point, and so forth.

Following is the XAML that demonstrates a *PolyLineSegment*:

```
<Path Stroke="Black">
    <Path.Data>
        <PathGeometry>
            <PathFigure StartPoint="100,100">
                <PolyLineSegment
                  Points="50,50,150,150,250,250,
                          100,200,200,100,300,300" />
            </PathFigure>
        </PathGeometry>
    </Path.Data>
</Path>
```

The *BezierSegment* Object

This object allows you to define a Bezier curve, which is a curve between two points defined by one or two control points. The *BezierSegment* object takes three points as parameters, called *Point1*, *Point2*, and *Point3*. Depending on how many you use, you get different behavior. So, for example, if you set *Point1* and *Point2*, the curve will be rendered from the start point to *Point2*, using *Point1* as the control point. If you set *Point1*, *Point2*, and *Point3*, the curve will be rendered from the start point to *Point3*, using *Point1* and *Point2* as control points.

Following is an example of a *PathFigure* containing a *BezierSegment*:

```
<Path Stroke="Black">
    <Path.Data>
        <PathGeometry>
            <PathFigure StartPoint="100,100">
                <BezierSegment Point1="140,120" Point2="100,140" />
```

```
        </PathFigure>
      </PathGeometry>
    </Path.Data>
</Path>
```

The *PolyBezierSegment* Object

This object allows you to set a group of points that Silverlight will interpret into a set of control points for a group of Bezier curves. Consider the following XAML:

```
<Path Stroke="Black">
  <Path.Data>
    <PathGeometry>
      <PathFigure StartPoint="100,100">
        <PolyBezierSegment>
          <PolyBezierSegment.Points>
            <Point X="50" Y="50" />
            <Point X="150" Y="150" />
            <Point X="250" Y="250" />
            <Point X="100" Y="200" />
            <Point X="200" Y="100" />
            <Point X="300" Y="300" />
          </PolyBezierSegment.Points>
        </PolyBezierSegment>
      </PathFigure>
    </PathGeometry>
  </Path.Data>
</Path>
```

Alternatively, you can define the set of points using a points collection stored as comma-separated values in a string:

```
<Path Stroke="Black">
   <Path.Data>
      <PathGeometry>
         <PathFigure StartPoint="100,100">
            <PolyBezierSegment  Points="50,50,150,150,250,250,
                                        100,200,200,100,300,300" />
         </PathFigure>
      </PathGeometry>
   </Path.Data>
</Path>
```

The result of this XAML is shown in Figure 2-21. To interpret this, the starting point is defined as being at position (100,100), which is the upper-left side of the overall curve. The first Bezier then goes to the end point (250,250), using (50,50) and (150,150) as control points. As these control points effectively cancel each other out (they are equidistant from the line from [100,100] to [250,250]), the first Bezier ends up being a straight line ending at (250,250). The second Bezier then starts at this point (250,250) and is drawn to the last point at (300,300), through control points at (100,200) and (200,100), which gives it the distinctive "loop back and then forward" look.

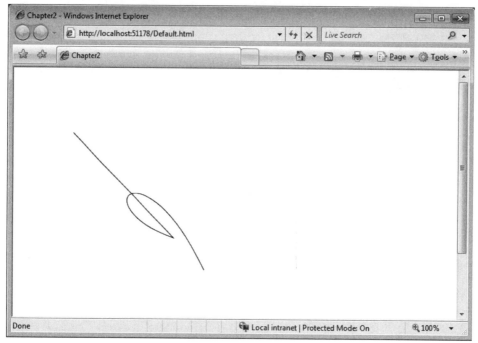

Figure 2-21   Using the *PolyBezierSegment*.

The *QuadraticBezierSegment* Object

A quadratic Bezier is a simple Bezier curve that is drawn as a regular quadratic curve using a single control point. It takes two point objects. If you only use one, it becomes the end point of the curve with no control point, and is effectively a straight line from the start point to the point you defined. If you use two points, then the second point is the end point of the curve, and the first is the quadratic control point. Here's an example:

```
<Path Stroke="Black">
   <Path.Data>
      <PathGeometry>
         <PathFigure StartPoint="100,100">
            <QuadraticBezierSegment Point1="200,0" Point2="300,100"  />
         </PathFigure>
      </PathGeometry>
   </Path.Data>
</Path>
```

This curve rendered by this XAML can be seen in Figure 2-22.

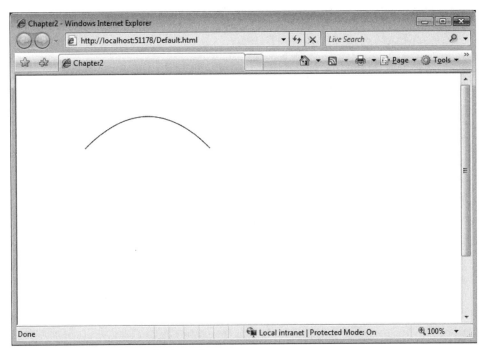

Figure 2-22   A simple quadratic Bezier curve.

The *PolyQuadraticBezierSegment* Object

As its name suggests, this is a collection of connected quadratic Bezier curves defined and parsed from a list of control points in a similar manner to that described for the *PolyBezierSegment* object earlier in this chapter. Following is an example of a *PolyQuadraticBezierSegment* in action:

```
<Path Stroke="Black">
    <Path.Data>
        <PathGeometry>
            <PathFigure StartPoint="100,100">
                <PolyQuadraticBezierSegment Points="50,50,150,150,250,250,
                                                    100,200,200,100,300,300" />
            </PathFigure>
        </PathGeometry>
    </Path.Data>
</Path>
```

The result of this XAML is shown in Figure 2-23.

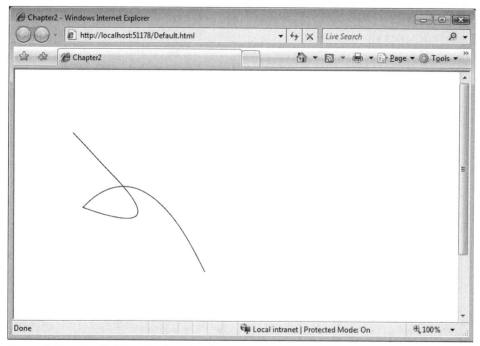

Figure 2-23 The *PolyQuadraticBezier* object in action.

This code draws a number of quadratic Bezier curves. The first is from the starting point, (100,100), to (150,150), with a control point at (50,50), which yields a straight line ending at (150,150). The second is then a curve starting at (150,150) and ending at (100,200), with a control point at (250,250). This is shown as the curve sweeping toward the left. The third curve then starts at (100,200) and ends at (300,300), through a control point at (200,100), and this is rendered as the long smooth curve going from left to right in Figure 2-23.

Compound Path Segments

Each of these segment types can be compounded within a *PathFigure* segment within a collection. Additionally, *PathFigure* segments can be collected within a *PathGeometry* to create a complex set of segments.

Following is an example where the *PathGeometry* contains two *PathFigure* objects. The first object has a *LineSegment*, a *PolyQuadraticBezierSegment*, and another *LineSegment*. The second object has a single *LineSegment*.

```
<Path Stroke="Black">
  <Path.Data>
    <PathGeometry>
      <PathFigure StartPoint="100,100">
        <LineSegment Point="200,200" />
        <PolyQuadraticBezierSegment Points="50,50,150,150,250,250,
                                    100,200,200,100,300,300" />
```

```
          <LineSegment Point="0,0" />
        </PathFigure>
        <PathFigure>
          <LineSegment Point="10,400" />
        </PathFigure>
      </PathGeometry>
    </Path.Data>
</Path>
```

Using the *GeometryGroup* Object

In the previous sections, you saw the various geometries that are available, from simple ones such as the *EllipseGeometry*, *LineGeometry*, and *RectangleGeometry*, to complex ones made up of many *PathSegments* within a *PathGeometry*. You can combine these together using a *GeometryGroup* object.

You simply define the geometries that you want as a collection within this object. Following is an example of a *GeometryGroup* containing an *EllipseGeometry*, a *RectangleGeometry*, and then the same complex *PathGeometry* that you used in the previous section:

```
<Path Stroke="Black">
  <Path.Data>
    <GeometryGroup>
      <EllipseGeometry RadiusX="100" RadiusY="100" Center="50,50" />
      <RectangleGeometry Rect="200,200,100,100" />
      <PathGeometry>
        <PathFigure StartPoint="100,100">
          <LineSegment Point="200,200" />
          <PolyQuadraticBezierSegment Points="50,50,150,150,250,250,
                                              100,200,200,100,300,300" />
          <LineSegment Point="0,0" />
        </PathFigure>
        <PathFigure>
          <LineSegment Point="10,400" />
        </PathFigure>
      </PathGeometry>
    </GeometryGroup>
  </Path.Data>
</Path>
```

Figure 2-24 shows how this will appear.

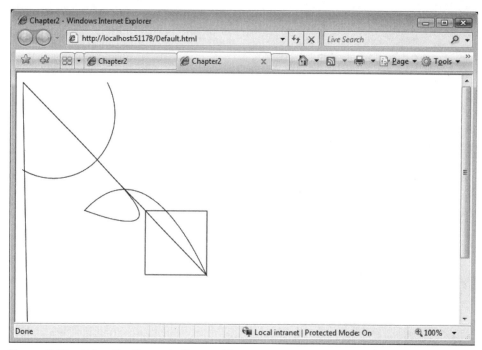

Figure 2-24 Using the *GeometryGroup* object to group many geometries together.

The *Path* Language

The *Path* object has a *Data* property that can use the *Path* language to define a complex path. This language uses the syntax of a command letter followed by a space, followed by a comma-separated list of numbers, followed by a space before the next command letter. Following is an example:

```
<Path Stroke="Black" Data="M 100,100 L 200,200" />
```

In this instance, the path is drawn using the *M* command, for *Move*, to move to (100,100) and the *L* command, for *Line*, to draw a line between there and (200,200).

- The *M* command places the drawing pen at the specified point without drawing a line between the current point and the defined point; that is, it moves the starting point. It will draw the line from (40,140) to (100,200), assuming there is no positioning on the parent canvas. If there is, Silverlight will draw the line relative to the parent positioning.

- The *L* (for Line) command draws a line from the current point to the specified point.

- The *H* command takes a single number as a parameter and draws a horizontal line between the current point and the specified value on the x-axis.

- The *V* command takes a single number as a parameter and draws a vertical line between the current point and the specified value on the y-axis.

- The *C* command takes three points as parameters. It draws a cubic Bezier curve between the current point and the third of these points, using the first two points as control points.

- The *Q* command takes two points as parameters and draws a quadratic Bezier curve between the current point and the second one, using the first as a control point.

- The *S* command takes two points as parameters and draws a smooth cubic Bezier curve between the current point and the second of these. It uses two control points—the current point itself and the first of the two parameters—to generate a smoother curve.

- The *T* command works in the same way as the *S* command, except that it draws a smooth quadratic Bezier curve.

- The *A* command takes five parameters—for size, rotation angle, *isLargeArc*, *sweepDirection*, and end point. It uses these parameters to draw an elliptical arc.

- The *Z* command ends the current path and closes it to form a closed shape by drawing a line between the current point and the starting point of the path.

Clipping and Geometries in XAML

XAML elements may be clipped according to a rule defined by a geometry. As we saw in the previous section, a geometry can be a simple geometry such as the *EllipseGeometry*, *LineGeometry*, or *RectangleGeometry*; a complex geometry defined using a *PathGeometry*; or a group of any of these contained within a *GeometryCollection*.

To define how an object is clipped, you simply set its attached *Clip* property to a geometry. The following example is an image being clipped by an *EllipseGeometry*:

```
<Image Source="smily.jpg" Width="300" Height="300"/>
<Image.Clip>
    <EllipseGeometry Center="150,150" RadiusX="100" RadiusY="100" />
</Image.Clip>
```

You can see how this looks in Figure 2-25.

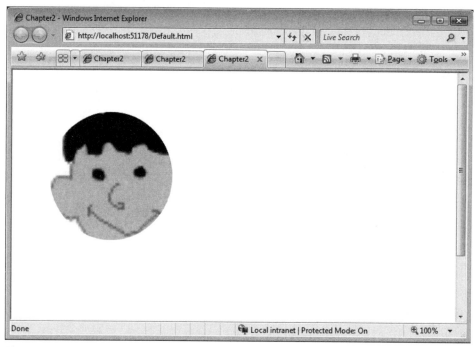

Figure 2-25 Clipping an image with a geometry.

XAML Controls in Silverlight

There are a number of XAML controls available to Silverlight developers. In Silverlight 1.0, these include the following:

- Canvas
- Image
- Glyphs
- TextBlock
- MediaElement

What we have seen so far in this chapter, properties such as clipping, brushes, layout, and more, apply to all of these elements. We will discuss the first four in the following subsections; the *MediaElement* control is covered in detail in Chapter 4.

The *Canvas* Element

This element defines an area of the page in which you can place child elements. It can be used to group elements visually, with their layout and positioning relative to the canvas. In addition, the *Canvas* object can be used solely as a container for other objects, allowing them to be treated as a single object with respect to placement and events handling.

Here's an example of collecting rectangles into groups using *Canvas* elements:

```
<Canvas Width="144" Height="128" Canvas.Left="24" Canvas.Top="8">
    <Rectangle Fill="#FF000000" Stroke="#FF000000"
                    Width="144" Height="64" Canvas.Top="24"/>
    <Rectangle Fill="#FF000000" Stroke="#FF000000"
                    Width="56" Height="128" Canvas.Left="40"/>
</Canvas>
<Canvas Width="152" Height="144" Canvas.Left="24" Canvas.Top="184">
    <Rectangle Fill="#FFFF0000" Stroke="#FF000000"
                    Width="152" Height="72" Canvas.Top="32"/>
    <Rectangle Fill="#FFFF0000" Stroke="#FF000000"
                    Width="64" Height="144" Canvas.Left="48"/>
</Canvas>
```

The *Image* Element

The *Image* element is used to define a graphic. This is set to the Universal Resource Indicator (URI) of a valid image, such as a bitmap, .jpg, .gif, or .png image.

Following is an example in which the layout of the image is set using *Height*, *Width*, *Canvas.Left*, and *Canvas.Top* properties, and the *Source* points to "smily.jpg":

```
<Image Width="184" Height="128" Canvas.Left="56" Canvas.Top="32" Source="smily.jpg"/>
```

The *Glyphs* Element

The *Glyphs* element is used to render fixed text according to a defined font. It can also be used to render characters that have no fixed keystroke associated with them, such as many graphics characters in fonts including Wingdings or Unicode text.

One thing to be careful about when using *Glyphs* is that for the glyph to work, the font will be downloaded to the target machine. As a result, you should ensure that you have distribution rights to the font that you are using.

To use the *Glyphs* element, you specify the font using the *FontUri* property. You then specify the characters to render using the *Indices* or *UnicodeString* properties. When using *Indices*, you specify characters based on their offset within the font definition using a semicolon-separated list.

In addition, you have to specify the font size using the *FontRenderingEmSize* property. Optionally, you can set the *StyleSimulations* property to emulate font styles. You can set this property to *BoldSimulation*, *ItalicSimulation*, or *BoldItalicSimulation*, as well as to the default setting, *None*.

Here's an example that uses two *Glyphs* elements. One uses the Wingdings font to draw some characters using their offset, and the other uses the Simhei font and Unicode to render some Chinese text.

> **Note** In order to run this application, you will need to have the webdings.ttf and simhei.ttf font files on your server in the same directory as the Silverlight application. If you don't have these fonts available, simply replace them with other fonts that you do have available. It is important to remember that if you use this technique in a production environment, you must have permission to distribute the fonts that you are using.

```
<Glyphs Canvas.Top="0" FontUri="webdings.ttf" Indices="133;134;135"
        Fill="Black" FontRenderingEmSize="48"/>

<Glyphs Canvas.Top="50" FontUri="simhei.ttf"
        UnicodeString="你好, 你好吗?" Fill="Black"
        FontRenderingEmSize="48"/>
```

You can see how this will be rendered by Silverlight in Figure 2-26.

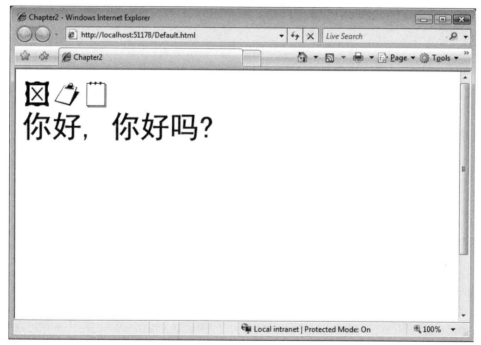

Figure 2-26 Using the *Glyphs* object.

The *TextBlock* Element

This is a lightweight object that displays single or multiline text with multiple formatting options. It differs significantly from the *Glyphs* element in that it does not require you to specify the font. Thus, regardless of the operating system or browser that you are using, the text will be rendered in the same way.

You specify the font family that you want the text to be rendered in using the *FontFamily* property. Silverlight supports nine basic fonts:

- Arial
- Arial Black
- Comic Sans MS
- Courier New
- Georgia
- Lucida Grande/Lucida Sans Unicode
- Times New Roman
- Trebuchet MS
- Verdana

The *FontSize* property is used to specify the size in pixels that you want the text to be rendered. The *FontStyle* property is used to determine the style that is rendered. This can be *Normal* or *Italic*.

The *FontWeight* property is used to determine the weight of the font when rendering. There are a number of possible values for this: *Thin*, *ExtraLight*, *Light*, *Normal*, *Medium*, *SemiBold*, *Bold*, *ExtraBold*, *Black*, or *ExtraBlack*.

The *TextDecorations* property is used to determine whether the text in the *TextBlock* is rendered with an underline or not. It can be set to *Underline* or *None*

The *TextWrapping* property is used to determine whether or not the *TextBlock* wraps the text. It can be set to *NoWrap*, so the text is on a single line and is clipped to the width of the *TextBlock*, or to *Wrap* so the text flows onto a new line when it goes beyond the available horizontal width. Text wrapping can affect the dimensions of the text box by changing the width through clipping the text and the height by adding extra lines. As a result, the default *Width* and *Height* properties may return an inaccurate value. So the *TextBlock* exposes *ActualWidth* and *ActualHeight* properties, which return the correct value.

Runs and Line Breaks

The *Run* element is used to change formatting or styling of text within a *TextBlock*. If you want a block of text to set with three different styles or fonts, you'd define the first style on the text block and set its text property to the desired text. You'd then add a run with the second style and text, and then add another run with the third style and its text. Here's an example:

```
<TextBlock FontFamily="Arial" Width="400"
        Text="ArialText">
<Run Foreground="Blue" FontFamily="Comic Sans MS"
    FontSize="24">Large Comic Sans</Run>
<Run Foreground="Teal" FontFamily="Verdana"
    FontSize="12" FontStyle="Italic">Italic Verdana</Run>
</TextBlock>
```

The text "ArialTextLarge Comic SansItalic Verdana" is then loaded into the *TextBlock*, but as "Large Comic Sans" is in a *Run* defined with one font and style, and "Italic Verdana" is defined in a different one, the rendered output will show the text as a single line with changing formats. You can see the results in Figure 2-27.

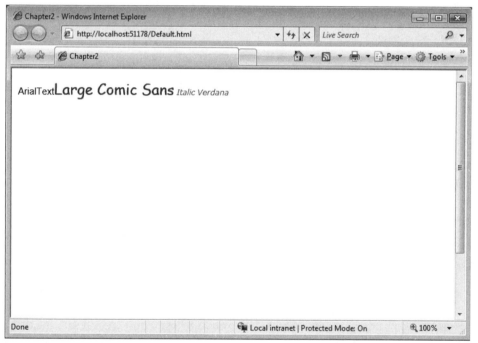

Figure 2-27 Using runs in your *TextBlock*.

You can create breaks in the text in your text block using the *LineBreak* element. This is simply inserted between runs to create a break. Following is the previous example updated to use a line break:

```
<TextBlock FontFamily="Arial" Width="400"
        Text="ArialText">
<Run Foreground="Blue" FontFamily="Comic Sans MS"
    FontSize="24">Large Comic Sans</Run>
  <LineBreak />
<Run Foreground="Teal" FontFamily="Verdana"
    FontSize="12" FontStyle="Italic">Italic Verdana</Run>
</TextBlock>
```

Figure 2-28 shows how this is rendered. You can see that the break appears between the words "Sans" and "Italic."

Figure 2-28   Using *LineBreak* in the *TextBlock*.

Summary

In this chapter, you learned about many of the details involved in setting up visual elements using XAML. You were introduced to layout, positioning, filling, strokes, opacity, paths, geometries, and clipping, which give you control over what you see in your user interface. In addition, you took a look at the generic controls that provide containment of controls and elements as well as text rendering.

In the next chapter, you'll examine how XAML is used to bring life to the user interface by adding transformations and animation!

Chapter 3
XAML: Transformation and Animation

In Chapter 2, "Silverlight and XAML," you learned how you can use XAML to render graphics on the screen, whether they are vector graphics, raster graphics (using the *Image* object), or video graphics. In this chapter, we will examine how to enhance these graphics using different types of transformations (to change how the object appears) and animations (to change attributes of the object over time). In addition, we'll introduce key frames and explain how they can be used to fine-tune animation behavior, and then we'll take a quick look at Expression Blend again, to see how it can be used to design animations visually.

Transformations

In graphics, a transform defines how to map points from one coordinate space to another. This is typically described using a *transformation matrix*, a special mathematical construct that allows for simple mathematical conversion from one system to another. Silverlight XAML abstracts this, and we will not go into detail about the mathematics in this book. Silverlight XAML supports four set transformations for rotation, scaling, skewing, and translation (movement), as well as a special transformation type that allows you to implement your own matrix, which is used to combine transformations.

Transformations are applied using transform properties. There are several different types of transform properties, which are applied to different object types.

Thus, when using a *Brush* type, you define your transformation using either the *Brush.Transform* property when you want to affect the brush's content—if you want to rotate an image before using it in an *ImageBrush*, for example—or you might use the *Brush.RelativeTransform* property, which allows you to transform a brush using relative values—something you might do if you are painting different areas of different sizes using the same brush, for example.

When using a *Geometry* type, you apply a simple transform using the *Geometry.Transform* property. This property does not support relative transforms.

Finally, when using a UI element, you specify the transformation to use with the *RenderTransform* property. If you are transforming an ellipse, for example, you'll use the *Ellipse.RenderTransform* to define the desired transform.

In the following section, we'll take a look at the different transformation types to see how these properties are used within their specific object types.

Rotating with the *RotateTransform* Property

RotateTransform allows you to rotate an element by a specified angle around a specified center point. You set the angle of rotation using the *Angle* property to set the number of degrees that you want to rotate the item. Consider the horizontal vector pointing to the right to be 0 degrees, and rotation takes place *clockwise*, so the vertical vector pointing down is the result of a 90-degree rotation.

You set the center of transformation using the *CenterX* and *CenterY* properties to specify the coordinates of the pivot. These default to 0.0, which makes the default rotation pivot the upper-left corner of the container.

Consider this example XAML, in which a *TextBlock* is rotated using a *RenderTransform* that contains a *RotateTransform* specifying a 45-degree rotation.

```
<TextBlock Width="320" Height="40"
        Text="This is the text to rotate" TextWrapping="Wrap">
    <TextBlock.RenderTransform>
        <RotateTransform Angle="45" />
    </TextBlock.RenderTransform>
</TextBlock>
```

You can see how this appears in Figure 3-1.

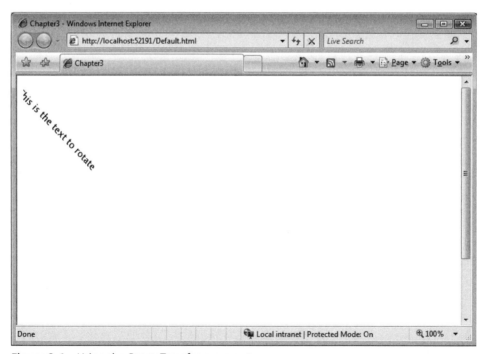

Figure 3-1 Using the *RotateTransform* property.

As you can see, this text is being rotated around a center point at (0,0)—at the upper-left corner of the screen.

This XAML shows how to use *CenterX* and *CenterY* to rotate around a different point. In this case, the rotation is done around the (100,200) point:

```
<TextBlock Width="320" Height="40"
         Text="This is the text to rotate" TextWrapping="Wrap" >
   <TextBlock.RenderTransform>
      <RotateTransform Angle="45" CenterX="100" CenterY="200" />
   </TextBlock.RenderTransform>
</TextBlock>
```

The results of this transformation are shown in Figure 3-2.

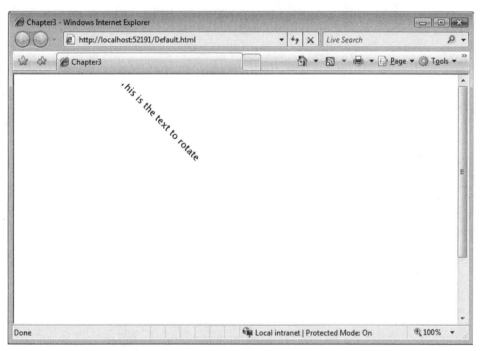

Figure 3-2   Rotating around a different center point.

Scaling with the *ScaleTransform* Property

The *ScaleTransform* property is used to change the size of an object based on the horizontal axis, the vertical axis, or both axes.

When scaling an object, you need to specify at least one of the axes around which you want to scale, and by how much you want to scale against that axis. You use the *ScaleX* property to scale the object on the horizontal axis, the x-axis, and the *ScaleY* to scale it on the vertical axis, the y-axis. These are set to a *double* value, which represents the value that you multiply the object's current size by on the specified axis. Therefore, values greater than 1 will stretch the object by that multiple. For example, using a *ScaleX* value of 2 will double the size of the object horizontally. Values less than 1 but greater than 0 will shrink the object. Using a setting of 0.5, for instance, will reduce the size of the object by half along the specific dimension.

So, for example, consider this XAML that creates a red rectangle 96 pixels wide by 88 pixels high:

```
<Rectangle Fill="#FFFF0404" Stroke="#FF000000" Width="96" Height="88"
Canvas.Left="112" Canvas.Top="72" />
```

Figure 3-3 shows what this looks like when it is rendered in Silverlight.

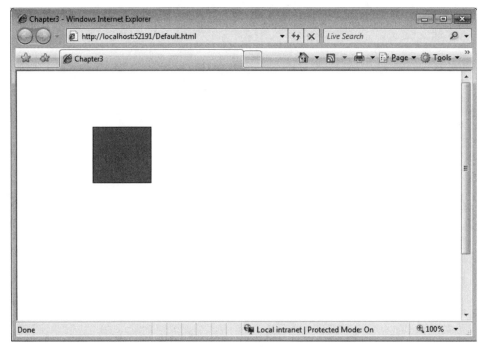

Figure 3-3   Rendering the rectangle in Silverlight.

To apply a *ScaleTransform* to this object, you use a *RenderTransform* and specify the transform to be a *ScaleTransform*. Here's the XAML:

```
<Rectangle Fill="#FFFF0404" Stroke="#FF000000"
        Width="96" Height="88" Canvas.Left="112" Canvas.Top="72">
  <Rectangle.RenderTransform>
    <ScaleTransform ScaleX="2" />
  </Rectangle.RenderTransform>
</Rectangle>
```

Figure 3-4 shows how this is rendered by Silverlight.

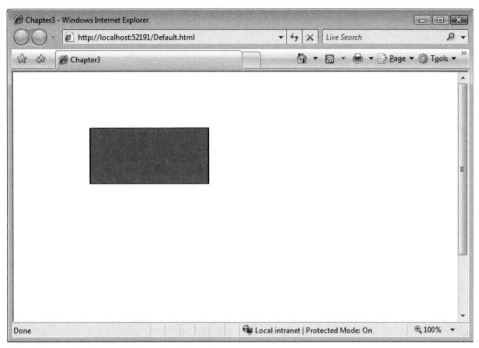

Figure 3-4   Scaling with the *ScaleTransform*.

You will notice that the rectangle increased in size horizontally to the right using this *Scale-Transform*. This was because the center of scaling was not specified. You can specify it with the *CenterX* property for horizontal scaling or the *CenterY* property for vertical scaling. These specify the coordinate of the center of scaling. This coordinate is relative to the upper-left corner of the rectangle. The coordinate default is 0, meaning that scaling will take place to the right on the horizontal axis and downward on the vertical axis.

If you set the *CenterX* property to a positive value (for example, 50), the scaling will be around the X point 50 pixels to the right of the leftmost side of the rectangle. This will make it look like the rectangle has moved a number pixels to the left of the one where the *CenterX* hasn't been changed (the number depends on the size of the scaling factor). This is because the stretching is centered on that point, pushing the left side of the rectangle to the left as well as pushing the right side to the right. You'll get similar effects by setting the *ScaleY* and *CenterY* values in the same way. Following is an example:

```
<Rectangle Fill="#FFFF0404" Stroke="#FF000000"
    Width="96" Height="88" Canvas.Left="80" Canvas.Top="80">
  <Rectangle.RenderTransform>
    <ScaleTransform ScaleX="2" CenterX="50"/>
  </Rectangle.RenderTransform>
</Rectangle>
```

You can see how this affects the rectangle in Figure 3-5.

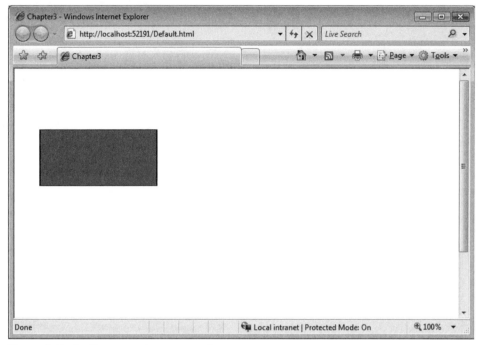

Figure 3-5 Scaling around a center point.

Moving an Object with the *TranslateTransform* Property

A *translation* is a transform that moves an object in a 2D plane from one position to another. It is defined by setting up vectors that define the object's motion along its x- and y-axes. These are set using the *X* and *Y* properties on the transform. To move an item two units horizontally (meaning it will move to the right), you set the *X* property to 2. To move it to the left, use a negative value, such as −2. Similarly, to move an object vertically, you would use the *Y* property, and positive values will cause the object to move down the screen, whereas negative values will move it up the screen.

Here's an example of a translate transform that moves the position of the red rectangle that we've been looking at by specifying *X* and *Y* values that move it up and to the left. These values effectively make up a *vector* that determines the transform.

```
<Rectangle Fill="#FFFF0404" Stroke="#FF000000"
          Width="96" Height="88" Canvas.Left="80" Canvas.Top="80">
  <Rectangle.RenderTransform>
    <TranslateTransform X="-50" Y="-50"/>
  </Rectangle.RenderTransform>
</Rectangle>
```

The results of this can be seen in Figure 3-6. As you can see, the rectangle has moved upward and to the left relative to its specified position, as compared to the position of the rectangle in Figure 3-3.

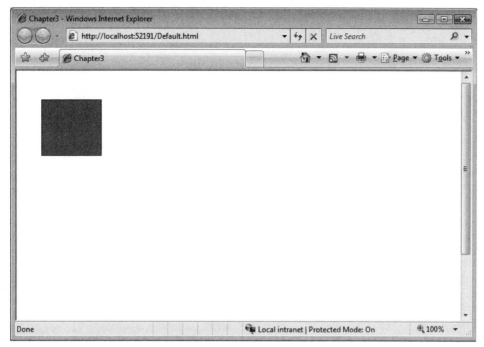

Figure 3-6   Using the *TranslateTransform* property.

Skewing an Object with the *SkewTransform* Property

Skewing an object involves changing it in a progressive, uniform manner along an axis. This has the effect of turning a square or rectangle into a parallelogram. This visual effect is very useful in creating the illusion of depth on a two-dimensional surface.

You can apply a skew at a certain angle on either the x- or y-axis and around a center point. These can, of course, be combined so that you can skew on both axes at the same time.

Following is the XAML that skews our rectangle on the x-axis by 45 degrees:

```
<Rectangle Fill="#FFFF0404" Stroke="#FF000000"
           Width="96" Height="88" Canvas.Left="80" Canvas.Top="80">
  <Rectangle.RenderTransform>
    <SkewTransform AngleX="45"/>
  </Rectangle.RenderTransform>
</Rectangle>
```

You can see the result of this in Figure 3-7.

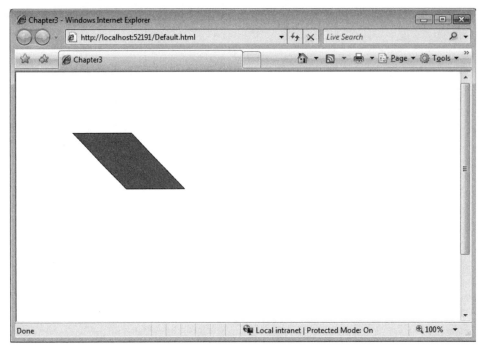

Figure 3-7   Skewing the rectangle using *SkewTransform*.

Simulating 3D Perspective with *SkewTransform*

Skewing is useful for simulating 3D effects in graphics. Following is an example of some XAML that uses three rectangles, two skewed on the x-axis and one on the y-axis, that create an illusion of a 3D perspective:

```
<Rectangle Fill="#FFFF0404" Stroke="#FF000000"
        Width="88" Height="88" Canvas.Left="80" Canvas.Top="80">
   <Rectangle.RenderTransform>
     <SkewTransform AngleX="45"/>
   </Rectangle.RenderTransform>
</Rectangle>
<Rectangle Fill="#FFFF0404" Stroke="#FF000000"
        Width="88" Height="88" Canvas.Left="80" Canvas.Top="168">
   <Rectangle.RenderTransform>
     <SkewTransform AngleX="45"/>
   </Rectangle.RenderTransform>
</Rectangle>
<Rectangle Fill="#FFFF0404" Stroke="#FF000000"
        Width="88" Height="88" Canvas.Left="80" Canvas.Top="80">
   <Rectangle.RenderTransform>
     <SkewTransform AngleY="45"/>
   </Rectangle.RenderTransform>
</Rectangle>
```

You can see the results of this in Figure 3-8.

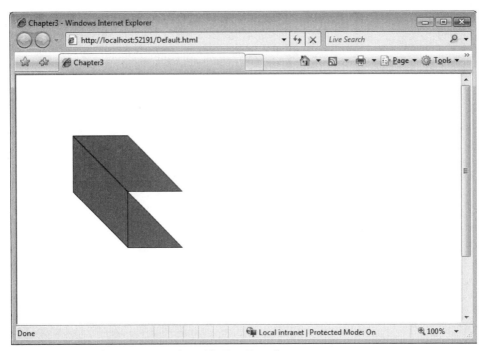

Figure 3-8 Simulating perspective with *SkewTransform*.

Defining Your Own Transforms with *MatrixTransform*

All transformations, at their heart, are performed by multiplying the coordinate space of the object by a transformation matrix. Each of the transforms that you've seen so far in this chapter is a well-known and well-defined transform.

Matrix mathematics and how transforms are implemented are beyond the scope of this book, but for the sake of syntactic completeness, we will look at how you can define them in Silverlight XAML.

Note that the matrix used in the *MatrixTransform* is an *affine* matrix, which means that the bottom row of the matrix is always set to (0 0 1), and as such you set only the first two columns. These are set using the transform's *Matrix* property, which takes a string containing the first two rows of values separated by spaces. Following is an example:

```
<Rectangle Fill="#FFFF0404" Stroke="#FF000000"
      Width="96" Height="88" Canvas.Left="80" Canvas.Top="80">
  <Rectangle.RenderTransform>
    <MatrixTransform Matrix="1 0 1 2 0 1" />
  </Rectangle.RenderTransform>
</Rectangle>
```

Figure 3-9 shows the impact of the transform using this matrix, which renders a combined stretched and skewed rectangle.

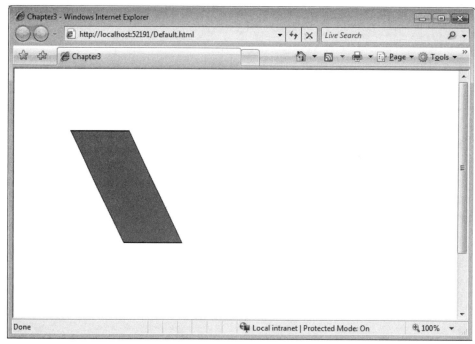

Figure 3-9   Using the *MatrixTransform*.

Combining Transformations

As you saw in the previous example, you can create a complex transformation by using its transformation affine matrix and specifying that using the *MatrixTransform* type. However, if you aren't an expert in matrix mathematics, another technique for using transforms is to combine them by means of the *TransformGroup* element. This simply allows you to specify multiple transforms, and the combined effect of each will be applied to the object. Here's an example:

```
<Rectangle Fill="#FFFF0404" Stroke="#FF000000"
        Width="96" Height="88" Canvas.Left="80" Canvas.Top="80">
    <Rectangle.RenderTransform>
      <TransformGroup>
         <ScaleTransform ScaleX="1.2" ScaleY="1.2" />
         <SkewTransform AngleX="30" />
         <RotateTransform Angle="45" />
      </TransformGroup>
    </Rectangle.RenderTransform>
</Rectangle>
```

This example combines a *ScaleTransform* that increases the size of the shape on both axes by 20 percent, with a 30-degree skew on the x-axis and a rotation of 45 degrees. You can see the results of this transformation in Figure 3-10.

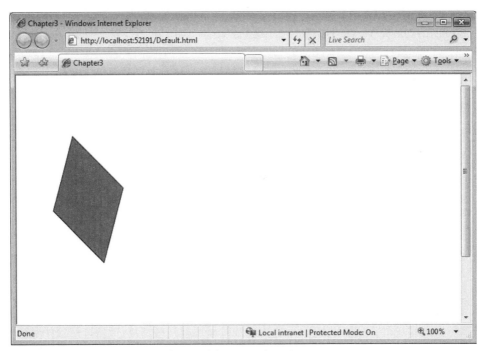

Figure 3-10   Combining transforms with a *TransformGroup*.

Animation

The word *animation* literally means "imparting life onto something." So, with animation you can bring your creations to life by changing the attributes of your objects, such as their color, size, opacity, and other properties, over time or in response to user actions.

In XAML, you animate an item by changing one or more of its properties over time. This time is defined using a timeline. So, for example, to move an item across the screen in 5 seconds, you'd specify a 5-second timeline that animates the *Canvas.Left* property from 0 to the width of the screen. In the next sections, we'll discuss each type of animation available, as well as the difference in animating these properties using key frames.

Before you look into the different animation types, you should know that there is a framework around animations that involves *Triggers*, *EventTriggers*, and *Storyboards*—first, let's take a look at these concepts, and then we'll examine the different animation types in more detail.

Using Triggers and Event Triggers

Animations in Silverlight take place in response to an event, which is defined using a trigger. At present, there is only one trigger type supported in XAML, the *EventTrigger*. Each UI property has a *Triggers* collection that is used to define one or more triggers (i.e., one or more *Event-Triggers*).

So, the first step in adding an animation to an element is to define its triggers collection, then you'll need to add at least one event trigger to the collection you've created. For example if you are animating a rectangle, the first step—specifying the triggers collection—will look like this:

```
<Rectangle x:Name="rect" Fill="Red" Canvas.Top="100"
          Canvas.Left="100" Width="100" Height="100">
   <Rectangle.Triggers>
   </Rectangle.Triggers>
</Rectangle>
```

Next, you will need to define an *EventTrigger* to add to this collection. On this *EventTrigger*, you will use the *RoutedEvent* property to specify the event to run the animation in response to. Chapter 5, "Programming Silverlight with JavaScript," has details on each event supported by each object in XAML, but in this case, the rectangle supports the following events: *Loaded*, *MouseEnter*, *MouseLeave*, *MouseLeftButtonDown*, *MouseLeftButtonUp*, and *MouseMove*.

To implement an animation that will begin when the rectangle is loaded, you would specify the *EventTrigger* as follows:

```
<EventTrigger RoutedEvent="Rectangle.Loaded">
</EventTrigger>
```

Then, the XAML snippet to run this animation looks like this:

```
<Rectangle x:Name="rect" Fill="Red" Canvas.Top="100"
          Canvas.Left="100" Width="100" Height="100">
   <Rectangle.Triggers>
     <EventTrigger RoutedEvent="Rectangle.Loaded">
     </EventTrigger>
   </Rectangle.Triggers>
</Rectangle>
```

The next step is to define the animation that you want to use. Animations are contained within *storyboards*, which are covered in the next section.

Using *BeginStoryboard* and *Storyboard*

BeginStoryboard is a trigger action that contains a *Storyboard* object. *Storyboard* objects contain the animation definitions. When you define an animation, you simply embed these objects within the *EventTrigger* definition. Here's how this would be accomplished using the rectangle example that we've been working with so far:

```
<Rectangle x:Name="rect" Fill="Red" Canvas.Top="100"
          Canvas.Left="100" Width="100" Height="100">
   <Rectangle.Triggers>
     <EventTrigger RoutedEvent="Rectangle.Loaded">
        <BeginStoryboard>
          <Storyboard>
          </Storyboard>
        </BeginStoryboard>
     </EventTrigger>
```

```
      </EventTrigger>
    </Rectangle.Triggers>
  </Rectangle>
```

Defining the Animation Parameters

Now that the framework for the animation is set up, you can specify the animation that you want to perform. At its most basic level, animation defines changing a property over a time duration. You can animate three different property types:

- Double types are animated using the *DoubleAnimation* or *DoubleAnimationUsingKey-Frames*. This method is used to animate properties that contain a *double* value—for example, dimensions such as *Canvas.Left*, or visual attributes such as *Opacity*.

- Point types are animated using a *PointAnimiation* or *PointAnimationUsingKeyFrames* type. This method is used to animate properties that contain a *Point* value, such as line segments or curves that are defined using points.

- Color types are animated using a *ColorAnimation* or *ColorAnimationUsingKeyFrames* type. This method is used to animate properties that contain a color value—the background or stroke of an element, for instance.

Each of these property types is animated from a value specified in the *From* attribute (or its current value if this is not set) either to a value specified in the *To* attribute or by a value specified in the *By* attribute.

Targeting the Animation

To define which object you want to apply the animation to, you use the *Storyboard.TargetName* property on these animation types, and you need to pass it the name of the object in question. Additionally, you specify the property that will be animated using the *Storyboard.TargetProperty*. Note that if you are specifying a complex or attached property (such as *Canvas.Left*), you place it in parentheses. So, for example, to specify a *double* animation to target the *Canvas.Left* of a rectangle named *rect*, the resulting XAML will look like this:

```
<DoubleAnimation Storyboard.TargetName="rect"
Storyboard.TargetProperty="(Canvas.Left)" ... />
```

Setting the Duration

To define how long it will take to transition the properties in question from one value to another, you use the *Duration* property. It is defined in the HH:MM:SS format, wherein a 5-second time duration for the animation is specified as 00:00:05, abbreviated to 0:0:5. Following is an example:

```
<DoubleAnimation Storyboard.TargetName="rect"
Storyboard.TargetProperty="(Canvas.Left)" Duration="0:0:5" ... />
```

Using the *AutoReverse* Property

Silverlight animation provides the facility to reverse the changes made as part of the animation. So, for example if you are moving a *double* value from 0 to 500 over a specific time frame, an *AutoReverse* will cause the animation to move from 500 back to 0.

Note that if the animation is set to run for 5 seconds as above, and the *AutoReverse* is set to *true*, and then the complete animation will take 10 seconds. Following is an example of XAML containing the *AutoReverse* property:

```
<DoubleAnimation Storyboard.TargetName="rect"
    Storyboard.TargetProperty="(Canvas.Left)" AutoReverse="True"
    Duration="0:0:5" ... />
```

Setting the *RepeatBehavior* Property

When the animation has finished running, there are a number of options you can apply to control how you want it to behave. These are specified using the *RepeatBehavior* property. This property can take three different types of values:

- A time defined in seconds. The timeline will wait for this period and then start the animation again.

- Constant repetition by setting *Forever* as the repeat behavior.

- A discrete number of repetitions by specifying a number followed by *x*, so, for example, if you want the animation to run three times, you specify the value 3x.

Following is the complete XAML for our animated rectangle to move it from 100 to 500 on the x-axis and then repeats that behavior three times:

```
<Rectangle x:Name="rect" Fill="Red"
    Canvas.Top="100" Canvas.Left="100" Width="100" Height="100">
  <Rectangle.Triggers>
    <EventTrigger RoutedEvent="Rectangle.Loaded">
      <BeginStoryboard>
        <Storyboard>
          <DoubleAnimation RepeatBehavior="3x"
                           Storyboard.TargetName="rect"
                           Storyboard.TargetProperty="(Canvas.Left)"
                           To="500" Duration="0:0:5"
                           AutoReverse="True" />
        </Storyboard>
      </BeginStoryboard>
    </EventTrigger>
  </Rectangle.Triggers>
</Rectangle>
```

Let's look at each of these animation types in a little more detail. First, we'll examine the attributes needed to animate each of the various types, and then we'll address where the associated key frame type of animation fits into the picture.

Animating a Value with *DoubleAnimation*

The *DoubleAnimation* object allows you to specify how a *double* value will change over a specified timeline. The animation is calculated as a linear interpolation between the property values over time.

When animating a *double*, you specify the value at the start of the animation using the *From* value, and then change it to either the *To* value, which is an absolute destination, or the *By* value, which is a relative destination.

For example, if you are moving the *Canvas.Left* property of an item from 100 (near the left of the screen) to 500, you can set *From* to 100 and *To* to 500, or *By* to 400. Note that if you set both, the *To* property takes precedence, and the *By* property is ignored. Also, if the rectangle is already located at the desired *From* position, you do not need to specify the *From* property.

The previous XAML example displayed this behavior. The rectangle is located with a *Canvas.Left* value of 100, and the *DoubleAnimation* specifies the *To* value as 500. Hence, the animation will move the value from 100 to 500, which will cause the rectangle to move across the screen to the right.

Animating a Color with *ColorAnimation*

ColorAnimation operates in a manner that is very similar to *DoubleAnimation*. You use it to specify how the color value will change over time. The animation is then calculated as a linear interpolation between the color values over the specified time.

When animating a color, you specify the value at the start of the animation using the *From* property. If you do not specify this, then the current color is used. You specify the desired end color using the *To* attribute. You can also specify a *By* attribute, which will provide the end color that is the result of adding the values of the *From* color (or the starting color) to the *By* color.

When you animate a color-based property, you do not animate the contents of the property directly, because the content of the property is usually a brush and not a color. So, if you want to animate the fill color of a rectangle, for example, you don't use the rectangle's *Fill* property as your target. Instead, you specify that you intend to animate the *Color* property of the *Solid-Brush* that is used to perform the fill.

Following is an example of how to animate the color of a rectangle, changing it from black to white over a time duration of 5 seconds, using a color animation:

```
<Rectangle x:Name="rect" Canvas.Top="100" Canvas.Left="100"
        Width="100" Height="100" Fill="Black">
  <Rectangle.Triggers>
    <EventTrigger RoutedEvent="Rectangle.Loaded">
      <BeginStoryboard>
        <Storyboard>
```

```
            <ColorAnimation Storyboard.TargetName="rect"
                            Storyboard.TargetProperty=
                              "(Shape.Fill).(SolidColorBrush.Color)"
                            To="#00000000" Duration="0:0:5" />
          </Storyboard>
        </BeginStoryboard>
      </EventTrigger>
    </Rectangle.Triggers>
</Rectangle>
```

As you can see, this XAML snippet specifies the *Color* property of the *SolidColorBrush* that is filling the shape as its target property. This is the typical XAML syntax used in addressing complex properties like this.

Animating a Point with *PointAnimation*

To change a value that is defined as a point over time, you use the *PointAnimation* type. The animation is then calculated as a linear interpolation between the values over the specified time.

In a manner similar to the *Color* and *double* animations, you specify the start value using *From* and the destination either as a relative direction (using *By*) or an absolute point (using *To*). Following is an example of how you could animate the end point of a Bezier curve:

```
<Path Stroke="Black" >
    <Path.Data>
        <PathGeometry>
            <PathFigure StartPoint="100,100">
                <QuadraticBezierSegment x:Name="seg"
                            Point1="200,0" Point2="300,100"  />
            </PathFigure>
        </PathGeometry>
    </Path.Data>
    <Path.Triggers>
        <EventTrigger RoutedEvent="Path.Loaded">
            <BeginStoryboard>
                <Storyboard>
                    <PointAnimation Storyboard.TargetName="seg"
                            Storyboard.TargetProperty="Point2"
                            From="300,100" To="300,600" Duration="0:0:5" />
                </Storyboard>
            </BeginStoryboard>
        </EventTrigger>
    </Path.Triggers>
</Path>
```

In this case, the Bezier curve is defined with a start point at (100,100), an end point at (300,100), and a control point at (200,0). An animation is set up to trigger after the path loads, and it animates the end point of the curve (*Point2*) from (300,100) to (300,600) over a time duration of 5 seconds.

Using Key Frames

The three animation types that you've just learned about, *ColorAnimation*, *DoubleAnimation*, and *PointAnimation*, all work by changing a defined property over time using linear interpolation. For example, if you are moving a double value from 100 to 500 over 5 seconds, it will increment by 80 each second.

Each of these can have this transition defined through a set of milestones called *key frames*. To change the linear behavior of the animation from the starting property to the ending property, you insert one or more key frames. Then you define the style of animation that you want between the various points.

Key frames are defined using *key times*. These are times that are specified relative to the start time of the animation, and they specify the end time of the key frame. So, imagine you need a 9-second animation with three evenly spaced key frames. Using key frames, you can specify the first key frame to end at 0:0:3, the second to end at 0:0:6, and the third to end at 0:0:9. You do not specify the *length* of the key time—instead, you specify the end time for each key frame.

As another example, consider a *double* animation that you want to span half the range of 100 to 500. The animation should move very quickly in the first half and very slowly in the second half, requiring a 6-second total transition. Since 350 is the midpoint between 100 and 500, you would define a key frame to begin at point 350. You'd tell it to go for 1 second between the start point and the midpoint, using a key time of 0:0:1, and then set a time duration of 5 seconds between the midpoint and the end point by using a second key time of 0:0:6. Now the item will zip across the screen to the midpoint and then will crawl the rest of the way.

In the previous example, both animated segments will be linearly interpolated. To provide extra flexibility, two other types of key frames are provided: a discrete key frame that instantly "jumps" the value between the two values, and a spline key frame that moves the value between the first and end points using a quadratic curve to define the interpolation. (In the following sections, you'll look at how to define an animation using key frames for the *double* type. The same principles apply for *Point* and *Color* animation types.)

To specify key frames, you use the *UsingKeyFrames* postfix on your animation. That is, to define *double* animations and use key frames, you'll use *DoubleAnimationUsingKeyFrames* on which you specify your target and property (in the same way you use *DoubleAnimation*). *DoubleAnimationUsingKeyFrames* contains the key frame definitions. (And as I mentioned, the same applies to *PointAnimationUsingKeyFrames* or *ColorAnimationUsingKeyFrames*.)

Using Linear Key Frames

The default method for animation between two property values is linear interpolation in which the amount is divided evenly over time. You can also define linear steps between frames using the *LinearKeyFrame* type in which linear interpolation is still used, but it is used between key frames, so you can have an acceleration/deceleration effect.

Consider the following animation. Here, a *DoubleAnimationUsingKeyFrames* is used, and it defines two key frames. One defines a linear interpolation between 0 and 300 for *Canvas.Left* changes over 1 second, and the next defines a linear interpolation between 300 and 600 for *Canvas.Left* changes over 8 seconds. This has the effect of making the rectangle move quickly to the halfway point and then slowly the rest of the way across. Similar principles apply for the *LinearPointKeyFrame* and *LinearColorKeyFrame*.

```
<Rectangle Fill="#FFFF0000" Stroke="#FF000000"
        Width="40" Height="40" Canvas.Top="40" x:Name="rect">
   <Rectangle.Triggers>
      <EventTrigger RoutedEvent="Rectangle.Loaded">
        <BeginStoryboard>
          <Storyboard>
            <DoubleAnimationUsingKeyFrames
                Storyboard.TargetName="rect"
                Storyboard.TargetProperty="(Canvas.Left)" >
              <LinearDoubleKeyFrame KeyTime="0:0:1" Value="300" />
              <LinearDoubleKeyFrame KeyTime="0:0:9" Value="600" />
            </DoubleAnimationUsingKeyFrames>
          </Storyboard>
        </BeginStoryboard>
      </EventTrigger>
   </Rectangle.Triggers>
</Rectangle>
```

Using Discrete Key Frames

If you want to change the property from one value to another and *not* use linear interpolation, you can use a discrete key frame. This causes the object to "jump" to the value at the specified key frame time. Following is the same example as the previous one, except that it uses a discrete key frame. At 1 second into the animation, the rectangle will jump halfway across the screen. Then at 9 seconds into the animation, it will jump to the right of the screen.

```
<Rectangle Fill="#FFFF0000" Stroke="#FF000000"
    Width="40" Height="40" Canvas.Top="40" x:Name="rect">
   <Rectangle.Triggers>
      <EventTrigger RoutedEvent="Rectangle.Loaded">
        <BeginStoryboard>
          <Storyboard>
            <DoubleAnimationUsingKeyFrames
                Storyboard.TargetName="rect"
                Storyboard.TargetProperty="(Canvas.Left)" >
              <DiscreteDoubleKeyFrame KeyTime="0:0:1" Value="300" />
              <DiscreteDoubleKeyFrame KeyTime="0:0:9" Value="600" />
            </DoubleAnimationUsingKeyFrames>
          </Storyboard>
        </BeginStoryboard>
      </EventTrigger>
   </Rectangle.Triggers>
</Rectangle>
```

Similar principles apply for the *DiscretePointKeyFrame* and *DiscreteColorKeyFrame*.

Using Spline Key Frames

To change the property from one value to another using a curved value that provides for acceleration and deceleration, you use a spline key frame. To do this, first you define a quadratic Bezier curve, and then the speed of the property as it moves from one value to another is determined by a parallel projection of that curve.

If this is hard to visualize, consider the following scenario: The sun is right overhead, and you hit a baseball into the outfield. You look at the shadow of the ball. As it is climbing into the air, the movement of the shadow appears to accelerate. As it reaches its apex, you'll see the shadow decelerate. As the ball falls, you'll see the speed of the shadow accelerate again, until it is caught or hits the ground.

Imagine your animation in this case is the ball's shadow, and the spline is the curve of the baseball. You define the trajectory of the baseball, a spline, using a *KeySpline*. The *KeySpline* defines control points for a quadratic Bezier curve. It is normalized so that the first point of the curve is at 0, and the second is at 1. For a parabolic arc, which is the trajectory the baseball would follow, the *KeySpline* will contain two comma-separated normalized values.

To define a curve like the flight of a baseball, you can specify the spline using a *KeySpline* such as 0.3,0 0.6,1. This defines the first point of the curve at (0.3,0) and the second at (0.6,1). This will have the effect of making the animation accelerate quickly until approximately one-third of the movement of the baseball is complete, then it will move at a uniform speed until approximately two-thirds of the ball's trajectory is reached, and then it will decelerate for the rest of the flight of the animated baseball, as the animation simulates the ball's fall to earth.

Following is an example of using a *KeySpline* to define the spline for this simulation using *DoubleAnimationUsingKeyFrames*:

```
<Ellipse Fill="#FF444444" Stroke="#FF444444"
        Width="40" Height="40" Canvas.Top="40" x:Name="ball">
    <Ellipse.Triggers>
        <EventTrigger RoutedEvent="Ellipse.Loaded">
            <BeginStoryboard>
                <Storyboard>
                    <DoubleAnimationUsingKeyFrames
                        Storyboard.TargetName="ball"
                        Storyboard.TargetProperty="(Canvas.Left)" >
                        <SplineDoubleKeyFrame KeyTime="0:0:5"
                            KeySpline="0.3,0 0.6,1" Value="600" />
                    </DoubleAnimationUsingKeyFrames>
                </Storyboard>
            </BeginStoryboard>
        </EventTrigger>
    </Ellipse.Triggers>
</Ellipse>
```

This example animates the ellipse so that it moves across the screen in a manner similar to the shadow of a baseball, as if you were above the baseball looking down toward the ground as the ball flies through the air.

Animation and Expression Blend

Animation can be defined graphically in Expression Blend. This generates the XAML for you to perform the animation, providing the different types of animation for you automatically.

When using Blend, press F7 or select Animation Workspace from the Window menu. This will give you the tools to graphically design timelines, and when you edit the properties that you want changed using the visual editor, then the XAML code for the animation will be generated. You can see this in Figure 3-11.

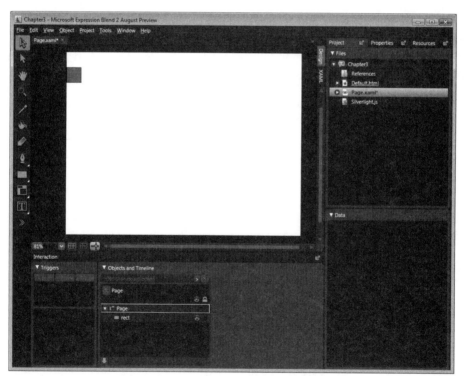

Figure 3-11   Expression Blend in Animation Workspace mode.

At the bottom of the screen, you can see the Objects And Timeline view. This allows you to add a timeline and then visually add key frames. To add a new timeline, click the > button in the Objects And Timeline view, and select the + button from the pop-up menu. See Figure 3-12.

Figure 3-12   Adding a new timeline.

When you click the + button, you'll see a dialog box that asks you for the name of the story-board to create. You can see the Create Storyboard dialog box illustrated in Figure 3-13.

Figure 3-13   Creating the storyboard.

When using Blend, animations are defined at the *Canvas* level. Animations then run in response to triggers on the canvas. Following is an example of the XAML created by Blend from the Create Storyboard dialog box:

```
<Canvas.Triggers>
   <EventTrigger RoutedEvent="Canvas.Loaded">
      <BeginStoryboard>
         <Storyboard x:Name="Timeline1"/>
      </BeginStoryboard>
   </EventTrigger>
</Canvas.Triggers>
```

The Objects And Timeline view will change to show the timeline that you've just created. You can see this in Figure 3-14.

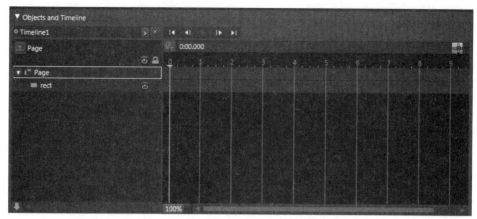

Figure 3-14   The Objects And Timeline view showing a new timeline.

The vertical line at time zero that you see in Figure 3-14 denotes the current time. (In Blend, this line will be yellow.) To add a key frame, you simply drag this line to the time where you want a key frame and click the Record Keyframe button. This button is located just above the timeline to the left of 0:00:000 in Figure 3-14.

Drag the line to the 4-second mark and add a key frame. You'll see the key frame added as a small oval on the timeline, as shown in Figure 3-15.

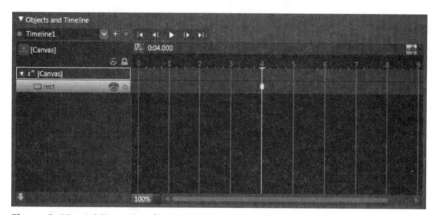

Figure 3-15   Adding a key frame.

Now that the timeline is on the 4-second frame and a key frame has been added, you can edit the rectangle's color, location, opacity, or shape, and Blend will calculate the correct transformations necessary to facilitate the animation. As an example, Figure 3-16 shows the same rectangle from Figure 3-11, but now it has been moved, filled with a different color, and resized.

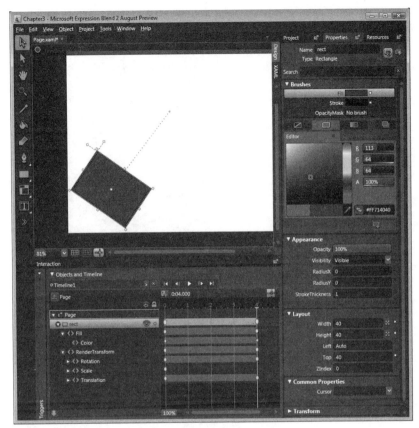

Figure 3-16   Specifying the key frame changes.

Finally, you may notice that if you drag the timeline indicator around, you can preview the animation and see how it appears at any particular time. Figure 3-17 shows how our rectangle appears at the 3-second key time, achieved by dragging the yellow line to the 3-second point.

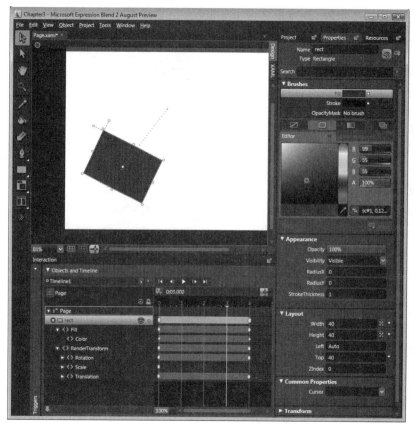

Figure 3-17   Previewing the animation.

Following is the complete XAML that was generated by Blend when designing this animation:

```
<Canvas.Triggers>
  <EventTrigger RoutedEvent="Canvas.Loaded">
    <BeginStoryboard>
      <Storyboard x:Name="Timeline1">
        <DoubleAnimationUsingKeyFrames BeginTime="00:00:00"
            Storyboard.TargetName="rect"
            Storyboard.TargetProperty="(UIElement.RenderTransform).
              (TransformGroup.Children)[3].(TranslateTransform.X)">
          <SplineDoubleKeyFrame KeyTime="00:00:04" Value="140"/>
        </DoubleAnimationUsingKeyFrames>
        <DoubleAnimationUsingKeyFrames BeginTime="00:00:00"
            Storyboard.TargetName="rect"
            Storyboard.TargetProperty="(UIElement.RenderTransform).
              (TransformGroup.Children)[3].(TranslateTransform.Y)">
          <SplineDoubleKeyFrame KeyTime="00:00:04" Value="20"/>
        </DoubleAnimationUsingKeyFrames>
        <ColorAnimationUsingKeyFrames BeginTime="00:00:00"
            Storyboard.TargetName="rect"
            Storyboard.TargetProperty="(Shape.Fill).(SolidColorBrush.Color)">
```

```
            <SplineColorKeyFrame KeyTime="00:00:04" Value="#FF000000"/>
          </ColorAnimationUsingKeyFrames>
          <DoubleAnimationUsingKeyFrames BeginTime="00:00:00"
              Storyboard.TargetName="rect"
              Storyboard.TargetProperty="(UIElement.RenderTransform).
              (TransformGroup.Children)[0].(ScaleTransform.ScaleX)">
            <SplineDoubleKeyFrame KeyTime="00:00:04" Value="2"/>
          </DoubleAnimationUsingKeyFrames>
          <DoubleAnimationUsingKeyFrames BeginTime="00:00:00"
              Storyboard.TargetName="rect"
              Storyboard.TargetProperty="(UIElement.RenderTransform).
              (TransformGroup.Children)[0].(ScaleTransform.ScaleY)">
            <SplineDoubleKeyFrame KeyTime="00:00:04" Value="2"/>
          </DoubleAnimationUsingKeyFrames>
        </Storyboard>
      </BeginStoryboard>
    </EventTrigger>
  </Canvas.Triggers>

<Rectangle Fill="#FFFF0000" Stroke="#FF000000"
      Width="40" Height="40" Canvas.Top="40" x:Name="rect"
      RenderTransformOrigin="0.5,0.5">
  <Rectangle.RenderTransform>
    <TransformGroup>
      <ScaleTransform ScaleX="1" ScaleY="1"/>
      <SkewTransform AngleX="0" AngleY="0"/>
      <RotateTransform Angle="0"/>
      <TranslateTransform X="0" Y="0"/>
    </TransformGroup>
  </Rectangle.RenderTransform>
</Rectangle>
```

Summary

In this chapter, you learned how transformations and animations are defined in Silverlight XAML. You were introduced to different types of transformation used to rotate, scale, or skew an object, as well as freeform transformations using an affine matrix as applied to a shape. You then learned about animations and saw how to define an animation to run based on a XAML trigger. You saw how animations change property values over time and looked at the XAML types that support animating double, point, and color values. You learned how to use key frames for finer control over your animations. Finally, you took a look at the Expression Blend animation designer to see how easily animations can be generated visually using Blend.

In the next chapter, you'll have a chance to examine how Silverlight 1.0 works with media—that is, how Silverlight can be used to implement video scenarios.

Chapter 4
Silverlight and Media

One of the most important uses for Silverlight 1.0 on the Web is to enable cross-platform, next-generation media. To accomplish this, Silverlight supports the *MediaElement* control. In this chapter, we'll look at the *MediaElement* in detail, and you will have a chance to work through a use case to build a simple media player that allows for progressive download and playback of videos. In addition to this, you'll learn how to paint surfaces with the video brush, which allows you to add interesting graphic effects.

The *MediaElement* control supports the following formats:

Video:

- WMV1: Windows Media Video 7

- WMV2: Windows Media Video 8

- WMV3: Windows Media Video 9

- WMVA: Windows Media Video Advanced Profile, non VC-1

- WMVC1: Windows Media Video Advanced Profile, VC-1

Audio:

- WMA7: Windows Media Audio 7

- WMA8: Windows Media Audio 8

- WMA9: Windows Media Audio 9

- MP3: ISO/MPEG Layer 3

- Mono or stereo

- Sampling frequencies from 8 to 48 KHz

- Bit rates from 8 to 320 KBps

- Variable bit rate

 Note Free format mode (as defined in ISO/IEC 11172-3) is not supported.

In addition to these formats, the *MediaElement* control also supports ASX playlists, as well as the *http*, *https*, and *mms* protocols.

When it comes to streaming video and/or audio, *MediaElement* supports live and on-demand streaming from a Windows Media Server. If the URI specifies the *mms* protocol, streaming is enabled; otherwise, the file will be downloaded and played back with progressive download, which involves downloading enough of the file to fill a playback buffer, at which point the buffered video is played back while the rest of the file is being downloaded.

If the protocol specifies the *http* or *https* protocols, then the reverse happens. *MediaElement* tries to progressively download first, and if this fails, the *MediaElement* control will attempt to stream the file.

Using the *MediaElement* Control

The *MediaElement* control is easy to get up and running in a basic setting, but it has many advanced features that can provide you with some pretty compelling scenarios when you have learned how to use them. But let's walk before we try to run and first step through how to do the most common tasks with the *MediaElement*.

Simple Video Playback with the *MediaElement* Control

To get started with the *MediaElement* control, add it to your page and set its *Source* attribute to the URL of the video that you want to play back. Following is an example:

```
<Canvas
  xmlns="http://schemas.microsoft.com/client/2007"
  xmlns:x="http://schemas.microsoft.com/winfx/2006/xaml"
  Background="White"
  >
  <MediaElement Source="balls.wmv"/>
</Canvas>
```

This will load and play back the media automatically. The *size* of the media is determined by the following rules:

- If the *MediaElement Height* and *Width* properties are specified, then the media element control will use them.

- If one of them is used, the media element control will stretch the media to maintain the aspect ratio of the video.

- If neither *Height* nor *Width* is set, the media element control will play back the video at its default size. If this is bigger than the Silverlight control's allotted viewing area, then the media element control will crop the video to fit the allotted viewing area.

Let's look at this by example. The balls.wmv video that is used in this chapter, and is available to download with the book code is a 480 × 360 video. If you instruct the *MediaElement* to show this video and do not set the *Height* and *Width* of the *MediaElement*, then the video will play back at 480 × 360. If your Silverlight component is 200 × 200, then you will see the pixels in the upper left 200 pixels of the video. You can see the portion of the video cropped in this way in Figure 4-1.

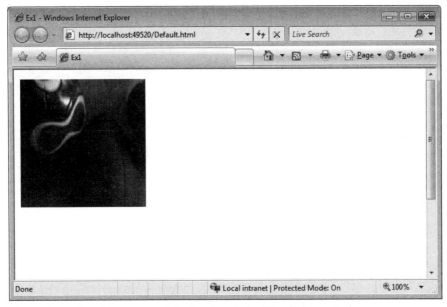

Figure 4-1   The video cropped to the size of the Silverlight control.

Controlling the Size of the *MediaElement* Control

As you saw in the previous section, the size of the *MediaElement* is important when determining how the video plays back. If the control does not have its size defined, and the video resolution is larger than the dimensions of the Silverlight control, it will be cropped.

To control the height and width of the *MediaElement* itself, you can use its *Height* and *Width* properties. When the control is rendered, the media will be stretched (or shrunk) or fit the media control. If the defined size of the media control is larger than the Silverlight control, then the media will be cropped to the size of the Silverlight control.

Following is an example of the *MediaElement* control set to 200 × 200, and Figure 4-2 shows how the video is rendered as a result.

```
<MediaElement Source="balls.wmv" Height="200" Width="200" />
```

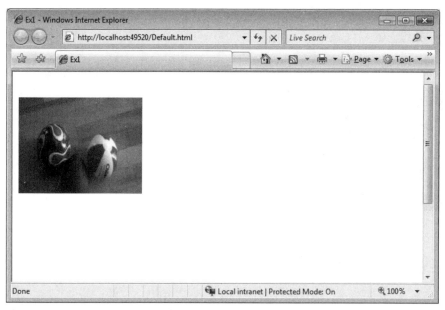

Figure 4-2   The video display after sizing the *MediaElement*.

Controlling How the Media Is Stretched

In the preceding example, the video has been stretched to fit the 200 × 200 *MediaElement*. As you can see in Figure 4-2, the video (which, as you recall, has a 480 × 360 pixel native resolution) is stretched to fit the dimensions while maintaining its aspect ratio. This yields black bars at the top and bottom of the video, giving the video a "letterbox" effect.

You can override this behavior using the *Stretch* property of the *MediaElement*. This property can take four different values:

- **None**   No stretching takes place. If the *MediaElement* is larger than the video, the video will be centered within it. If it is smaller, the center portion of the video will be shown. For example, the video is 480 × 360. If the *MediaElement* is 200 × 200 and *Stretch* is set to *None*, the center 200 × 200 area of the video will be displayed, as shown in Figure 4-3.

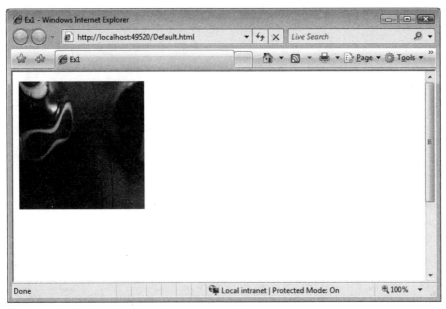

Figure 4-3   Setting the *Stretch* property to *None*.

- **Uniform**   This is the default stretching mode, and it maintains the video's aspect ratio and adds black bars at the top, bottom, or sides to maintain it, as we saw in Figure 4-2 previously.

- **UniformToFill**   This stretches the video, maintaining the aspect ratio but cropping the video to fit the window. So, for example, if the video is wider than it is high (e.g., 480 × 360) and it is stretched to accommodate a 200 × 200 window, the sides of the video will be cropped to fit the allotted viewing window (a smaller square, in this case). You can see how this affects the video display in Figure 4-4. If you compare the image in Figure 4-4 to the same frame of video shown in Figure 4-2, you can see how it is cropped on both sides.

- **Fill**   This stretch mode fills the *MediaElement* with the video, distorting the aspect ratio if necessary. Figure 4-5 shows the video when *Stretch* is set to *Fill*. As you can see in this case, the video has been stretched vertically to fill the paint area.

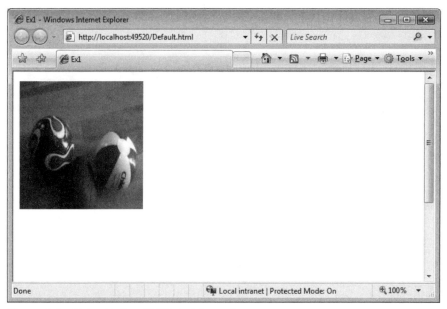

Figure 4-4 Using *UniformToFill* stretch mode.

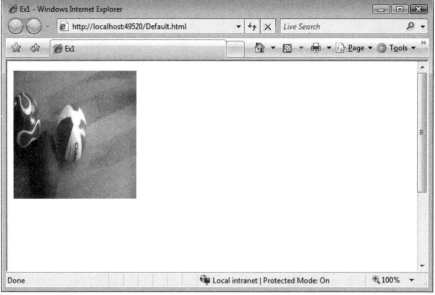

Figure 4-5 Using *Stretch* set to *Fill*.

Controlling Video Opacity

You can control the opacity of the *MediaElement* by using the *Opacity* property. This contains a normalized value, with 0 equal to totally invisible, 1 equal to completely visible, and everything in between representing different levels of opacity. The video will be rendered with this opacity and items behind the media element will become visible.

Following is an example of some XAML with a red rectangle and a *MediaElement*. The *MediaElement* is set to 0.5 opacity, which will make the video appear semitransparent. Because the *MediaElement* is rendered second, it is placed higher in the Z-order and thus it is rendered on top of the rectangle. Figure 4-6 shows the result of this example on the video display.

```
<Rectangle Fill="Red" Height="100" Width="200" />
<MediaElement Source="balls.wmv" Height="200"
        Width="200" Stretch="Fill" Opacity="0.5" />
```

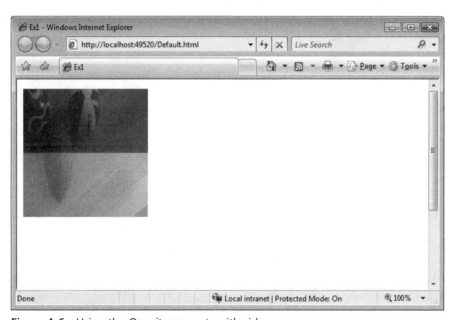

Figure 4-6   Using the *Opacity* property with video.

Using Transformations with the *MediaElement* Control

Chapter 3, "XAML: Transformation and Animation," described transformations in detail, but one of the nice things about the *MediaElement* is that you can use it to perform transformations, and the video that you are rendering will also be transformed. This can lead to some very nice effects. For example, the following is a *MediaElement* with a skew transform applied:

```
<MediaElement Source="balls.wmv" Height="200" Width="200" Stretch="Fill" >
    <MediaElement.RenderTransform>
        <SkewTransform AngleX="45"/>
    </MediaElement.RenderTransform>
</MediaElement>
```

You can see how this appears in Figure 4-7.

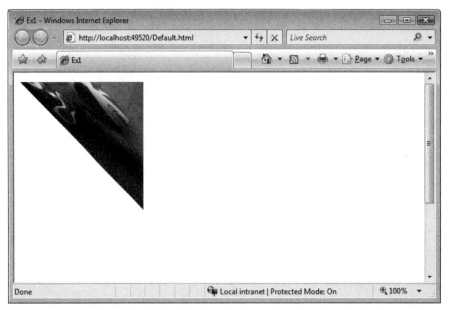

Figure 4-7   Skewing video with *SkewTransform*.

Writing Content on Video

Silverlight allows you to place content, including text and graphics, on top of video with ease. You can either place it using *ZOrder* properties on UI elements (see Chapter 1, "Introducing Silverlight"), or you can simply place UI elements in the same space as the media element and declare them later in the XAML. Following is an example of a *MediaElement* that has a *Canvas* containing a rectangle and text block that overlays the video.

```
<MediaElement Source="balls.wmv" Height="200" Width="200" Stretch="Fill" />
<Canvas Canvas.Top="140" Canvas.Left="20">
    <Rectangle Fill="Red" Height="40" Width="160" />
    <TextBlock>Subtitle on Video</TextBlock>
</Canvas>
```

Figure 4-8 shows how this will be rendered.

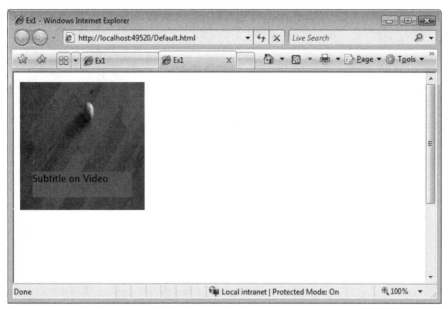

Figure 4-8   Rendering content on top of video.

Clipping Media with Geometries

Chapter 2, "Silverlight and XAML," introduced clipping and geometries. These also apply to a *MediaElement*, where you can define a geometry using shapes or paths and set this to be the clipping geometry for the *MediaElement* you're working with. So, for example, this XAML defines an ellipse as the clip region for our *MediaElement*:

```
<MediaElement Source="balls.wmv" Height="200" Width="200" Stretch="Fill" >
   <MediaElement.Clip>
      <EllipseGeometry RadiusX="100" RadiusY="75" Center="100,75"/>
   </MediaElement.Clip>
</MediaElement>
```

You can see the results of this in Figure 4-9.

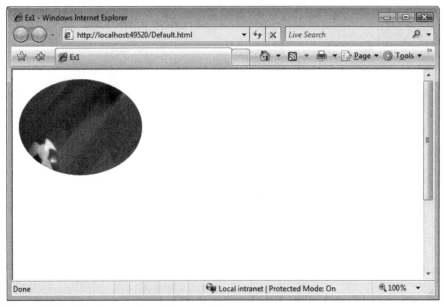

Figure 4-9   Clipping media with geometries.

Determining Automatic Playback Behavior

The default behavior for the *MediaElement* after its source is set is to have the media play back automatically. This can be controlled using the *AutoPlay* property. This defaults to *true*, but you can override this by setting it to *false*. You can play back the media later using its *Play* method. This and the other methods and events that you can use in programming the media element are shown in the next section.

Controlling Audio

You can use the *MediaElement* control's *IsMuted* property to set the audio to accompany the playback or not. This property is a Boolean value, and if you set it to *true*, no audio will be heard.

Additionally, you can control the volume of the audio using the *Volume* property. This is a normalized value with 0 equal to no audio, 1 equal to full volume, and values in between representing the relative volume. So, for example, 0.43 would set the volume to play at 43 percent of its full capacity.

Finally, the balance of the audio can be controlled with the *Balance* property. This symbol is set with a value between −1 and +1. A value of −1 will cause the audio to be panned all the way to the left—that is, the left speaker will play the audio at 100 percent volume, and the right speaker will play no audio, or 0 percent volume. A value of +1 will cause just the opposite to happen—the audio will be panned all the way to the right, with the right speaker playing the audio at 100 percent volume. A value of 0 causes the volume to be distributed evenly between the two speakers.

As an example, if the *Balance* property is set to a value of 0.8, then the right speaker will play the audio at 80 percent volume and the left speaker will play it at 20 percent volume. If the value −0.8 is used, the left speaker will play the audio at 80 percent volume and the right speaker will play the audio at 20 percent volume.

Following is some XAML specifying that the audio is not muted, that the master volume is at 50 percent, and that the audio is balanced towards the right speaker:

```
<MediaElement x:Name="vid" Source="balls.wmv" Height="200" Width="200"
    Stretch="Fill" IsMuted="False" Volume="0.5" Balance="0.8" />
```

Programming the *MediaElement*

The *MediaElement* offers a rich programming model that allows you to control playback with play, stop, and pause methods. It also allows you to respond to the video, capturing the buffering and download progress as well as responding to markers placed within the video. You also can specify events to trap such as mouse behavior.

Providing Basic Video Controls

The basic video control methods available are *Play*, *Stop*, and *Pause*. When you set the *AutoPlay* property of the *MediaElement* to *false*, then these controls are necessary to start playing the video. Even if *AutoPlay* is set to *true* and the video starts playing, then you can stop or pause it with these methods.

Following is an example of a XAML containing a media element and three simple video playback controls, implemented as *TextBlock* elements:

```
<MediaElement x:Name="vid" Source="balls.wmv" Height="200" Width="200" Stretch="Fill" />
<Canvas Canvas.Top="160">
    <Rectangle Fill="Black" Width="200" Height="24" Opacity="0.7"/>
    <TextBlock Foreground="White" Canvas.Left="20">Play</TextBlock>
    <TextBlock Foreground="White" Canvas.Left="80">Stop</TextBlock>
    <TextBlock Foreground="White" Canvas.Left="140">Pause</TextBlock>
</Canvas>
```

Figure 4-10 shows how the controls will appear on the video.

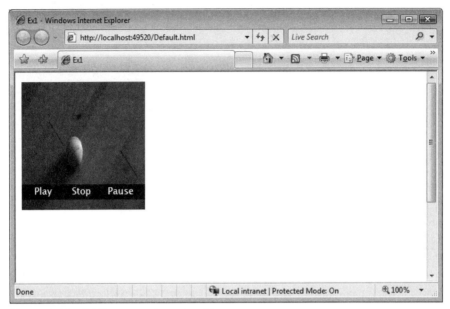

Figure 4-10 Adding controls to the video.

To create the controls, you specify the name of the code function that should run in response to a mouse event using an attribute of the video control element itself. You'll find much more detail about handling Silverlight events in Chapter 5, "Programming Silverlight with JavaScript." However, in this case, we simply want the video to start, stop, or pause when the user clicks on the appropriate text block. This is achieved by handling the *MouseLeftButton-Down* event, exhibited by the text block, that is hooked to functions that will play, pause, or stop the media element.

These functions need to be accessible from the page hosting the Silverlight control. So, they can either be implemented using JavaScript elements on the page, or within a .js file that is included on the page using the JavaScript element with its *Src* property set accordingly.

If you're using Expression Blend to put together your XAML content, it provides pseudo code-behind files for Default.html (it is named Default.html.js) and Scene.xaml (it is named Scene.xaml.js). These are an ideal location to implement your JavaScript functionality.

Following is the XAML that defines the same UI that was created in the previous example, but with event handler declarations added.

```
<MediaElement x:Name="vid" Source="balls.wmv"
              Height="200" Width="200" Stretch="Fill" />
<Canvas Canvas.Top="160">
   <Rectangle Fill="Black" Width="200" Height="24" Opacity="0.7"/>
   <TextBlock MouseLeftButtonDown="doPlay"
              Foreground="White"
              Canvas.Left="20">Play</TextBlock>
   <TextBlock MouseLeftButtonDown="doStop"
```

```
                Foreground="White"
                Canvas.Left="80">Stop</TextBlock>
    <TextBlock MouseLeftButtonDown="doPause"
                Foreground="White"
                Canvas.Left="140">Pause</TextBlock>
</Canvas>
```

Now you can write JavaScript to play, stop, and pause the video. Here's the code:

```
function doPlay(sender, args)
{
  var meVid = sender.findName("vid");
  meVid.Play();
}

function doStop(sender, args)
{
  var meVid = sender.findName("vid");
  meVid.Stop();
}

function doPause(sender, args)
{
  var meVid = sender.findName("vid");
  meVid.Pause();
}
```

When you define a JavaScript function as an event handler, it should take two parameters. The first, *sender*, is an object that represents the object that raised the event. The second, *args*, contains arguments that are included as part of the event.

Now, within this JavaScript function you'll have to get a reference to the *MediaElement* object that you are controlling. You do this using the *findName* method of the sender. The sender is the parent *Canvas*, so executing its *findName* method will search through its children until it finds an element called vid (which we established using the *x:Name* attribute as applied to our *MediaElement* object). If you look back to the XAML, you'll see that the *MediaElement* had an *x:Name* value of *vid*, so this should succeed. You'll be given a reference to the corresponding *MediaElement* object in a JavaScript variable called *meVid*. You can now simply invoke the *Play*, *Stop*, or *Pause* methods on this to control the video.

Managing Buffering and Download

When using progressive video download, the media infrastructure determines how much video it needs to cache before it can start playing back the video. So, depending on the bandwidth required to serve the video and the bandwidth available, it creates a buffer to hold enough video so that it can start playing back the video while it is downloading video to the buffer in the background.

When the buffer is 100 percent full, the video will begin playing back. Video may pause momentarily as network conditions change and the buffer is refilled. Silverlight allows you to monitor this behavior with the *BufferingProgressChanged* event and the *BufferingProgress* property. You can use this to provide status to your users as to the current buffering status, or to run logic to improve your UX as a result of buffering conditions. So, for example, you may have a poor connection, and buffering may never improve to above 50 percent. You can trap this value and provide the appropriate feedback to your client.

To manage buffering, hook an event handler to your *MediaElement* that defines a JavaScript function to handle the *BufferingProgressChanged* event like this:

```
<MediaElement x:Name="vid" Source="balls.wmv" Height="200" Width="200"
      Stretch="Fill" BufferingProgressChanged="doBuff"/>
<TextBlock x:Name="txtBuff"></TextBlock>
```

This specifies that a JavaScript function called *doBuff* will run whenever the buffering progress changes. This event goes hand in hand with the *BufferingProgress* property. This property contains a value from 0 to 1, where 0 is an empty buffer and 1 is a full buffer. The event will fire when the buffer changes by 5 percent (i.e., 0.05) or more, and when it is full.

Following is code that you can use to handle in response to this event firing that provides feedback on the current state of the buffer to your users:

```
function doBuff(sender, args)
{
    var theText = sender.findName("txtBuff");
    var meVid = sender.findName("vid");
    var prog = meVid.BufferingProgress * 100;
    prog = "Buffering % " + prog;
    theText.Text = prog;
}
```

You can override the automatic buffer by setting a specific buffer time. So, if you want to control the video buffering process so that you'll always have a 10-second buffer of video and thereby reduce your risk of paused video while buffers resynchronize in bad network conditions, you can set the *BufferingTime* property. You set this using a time span. To apply a 10-second buffer, for example, you specify the *BufferingTime* as 0:0:10, as shown in the following example:

```
<MediaElement x:Name="vid" Source="balls.wmv" Height="200" Width="200"
      Stretch="Fill" BufferingProgressChanged="doBuff" BufferingTime="0:0:10"/>
<TextBlock x:Name="txtDown"></TextBlock>
```

When progressive download isn't available or supported, the entire video file needs to be downloaded before it can be played back. In this case, the *DownloadProgressChanged* event and *DownloadProgress* property can be used to provide the status of the download. You use these in the same manner as the buffering functions. Following is XAML that defines a *DownloadProgressChanged* event:

```
<MediaElement x:Name="vid" Source="balls.wmv" Height="200" Width="200"
    Stretch="Fill" BufferingProgressChanged="doBuff"
    BufferingTime="0:0:10" DownloadProgressChanged="doDown"/>
```

And here is the code for the *doDown* function that defines the event handler:

```
function doDown(sender, args)
{
   var theText = sender.findName("txtDown");
   var meVid = sender.findName("vid");
   var prog = meVid.DownloadProgress * 100;
   prog = "Downloading % " + prog;
   theText.Text = prog;
}
```

Managing Current Video State

Silverlight presents a *CurrentState* property and an associated *CurrentStateChanged* event that can be used to respond to changes in state of the media.

The valid states for the *CurrentState* property are:

- **Buffering**   The buffer is less than 100 percent full, so the media is in a paused state while the buffer fills up.
- **Closed**   The media has been closed.
- **Error**   There is a problem downloading, buffering, or playing back the media.
- **Opening**   The media has been found and buffering or downloading is about to begin.
- **Paused**   The media has been paused.
- **Playing**   The media is being played back.
- **Stopped**   The media has been stopped.

Here's how you specify the *MediaElement*'s *CurrentStateChanged* event in XAML:

```
<MediaElement x:Name="vid" Source="balls.wmv" Height="200" Width="200"
    Stretch="Fill" CurrentStateChanged="doState" BufferingTime="0:0:10" />
```

This specifies a *doState* function to call in response to the changing current state. Following is a sample JavaScript function that runs as a result of this, using the *CurrentState* property of the *MediaElement* in an alert string:

```
function doState(sender, args)
{
   var meVid = sender.findName("vid");
   alert(meVid.CurrentState);
}
```

Managing Playback Position

You can use the *NaturalDuration* and *Position* properties of the media element to control its current playback position status. After the media's *CurrentState* property is set to *Opened*, then the *NaturalDuration* property will be set. This will report the length of the video in seconds using the *NaturalDuration.Seconds* property. You can then use JavaScript to convert this to hours, minutes, and seconds.

In this example, the *MediaElement* has its *CurrentStateChanged* event wired up to the *doState* JavaScript function (from the previous example). However, the function now captures the *NaturalDuration* property and uses the *convertDT* JavaScript helper function to format this as a string. Following is the JavaScript code:

```
function doState(sender, args)
{
   var meVid = sender.findName("vid");
   var txtStat = sender.findName("txtStat");
   var datetime = new Date(0, 0, 0, 0, 0, meVid.naturalDuration.Seconds)
   durationString = convertDT(datetime);
   txtStat.Text = durationString.toString();
}

function convertDT(datetime)
{
   var hours = datetime.getHours();
   var minutes = datetime.getMinutes();
   var seconds = datetime.getSeconds();
   if (seconds < 10) {
        seconds = "0" + seconds;
   }

   if (minutes < 10) {
        minutes = "0" + minutes;
   }

   var durationString;
   if (hours > 0) {
        durationString = hours.toString() + ":" + minutes + ":" + seconds;
   }
   else {
        durationString = minutes + ":" + seconds;
   }
   return durationString;
}
```

You can report on the current position of the video using the *Position* property. In this example, the position is reported on the status screen when the video is paused. It uses the same JavaScript helper function as we saw earlier.

```
function doPause(sender, args)
{
   var meVid = sender.findName("vid");
   meVid.Pause();
   var txtStat = sender.findName("txtStat");
   var datetime = new Date(0,0,0,0,0, meVid.Position.Seconds);
   positionString = convertDT(datetime);
   txtStat.Text = positionString.toString();
}
```

Using Media Timeline Markers

A timeline marker is a piece of metadata that is associated with a particular point in a media timeline. They are usually created and encoded into the media ahead of time using software such as Expression Media, and they are often used to provide chapter stops in video.

Silverlight supports these markers so that when it reaches a marker on the timeline as it is playing back media, it raises the *MarkerReached* event. You can catch this event and process it to trigger actions upon hitting the mark.

Following is an example of a XAML snippet that specifies the event handler for reaching a marker using the *MarkerReached* attribute. It specifies a JavaScript function called *handleMarker* as the event handler:

```
<MediaElement x:Name="vid" Source="balls.wmv" Height="200" Width="200"
MarkerReached="handleMarker" />
```

The arguments raised by this event contain a *marker*. This contains a *TimeSpan* object containing the time of the marker. The previous section, "Managing Playback Position," provides an example showing how to format a *TimeSpan* object into a friendly string. It also contains a *Type* property for the marker, which is a string that is defined by the person performing the encoding. Finally, it contains a *Text* parameter that allows for free format text and is usually used to describe the parameter. Following is the JavaScript to capture all three and build a string that is rendered using an alert box:

```
function handleMarker(sender, args)
{
   var strMarkerStatus = args.marker.time.seconds.toString();
   strMarkerStatus += "  :  ";
   strMarkerStatus += args.marker.type;
   strMarkerStatus += "  :  ";
   strMarkerStatus += args.marker.text;
   alert(strMarkerStatus);
}
```

You can see how this looks in Figure 4-11.

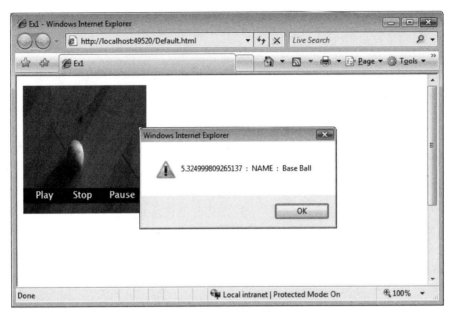

Figure 4-11   Capturing timeline markers in Silverlight.

You can also dynamically add timeline markers to your media file using JavaScript in Silverlight. This can be used to create chapter stops as a percentage of the length of the file, for example.

Following is an example in which the XAML for the *MediaElement* defines the JavaScript function *handleOpen* to fire when the media is opened. This inserts a new timeline object into the video at the 10-second position. This element is not permanently stored in the video, and it is lost when the session ends.

```
<MediaElement x:Name="vid" Source="balls.wmv"
    Height="200" Width="200"
    MarkerReached="handleMarker"
    MediaOpened="handleOpened" />
```

The JavaScript handler then creates a new timeline element in XAML and appends it to the *MediaElement*'s marker collection. This sets up a timeline marker at 10 seconds, with the *Type* set to 'My Temp Marker' and the *Text* set to 'Dynamically Added Marker Marker':

```
function handleOpened(sender, args)
{
   var marker =
   sender.getHost().content.createFromXaml("<TimelineMarker Time='0:0:10'" +
      " Type='My Temp Marker' Text='Dynamically Added Marker Marker' />");
   sender.markers.add(marker);
}
```

Now, when the *MediaElement* reaches the 10-second point on the playback, the alert dialog box shown in Figure 4-12 is raised.

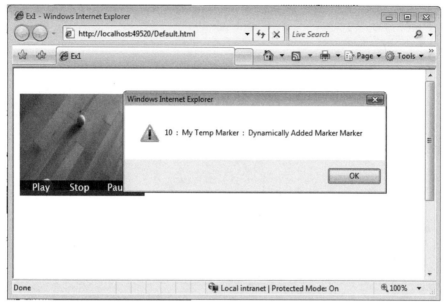

Figure 4-12   Using a dynamically added marker.

Finally, you can also set markers ahead of time by defining them in the XAML as a part of the *Media Element*'s markers collection. Here's the XAML for this:

```
<MediaElement x:Name="vid" Source="balls.wmv"
        Height="200" Width="200" MarkerReached="handleMarker">
   <MediaElement.Markers>
      <TimelineMarker Time='0:0:10' Type='My Temp Marker'
             Text='Dynamically Added XAML Marker' />
   </MediaElement.Markers>
</MediaElement>
```

Painting Video Using the *VideoBrush*

A particularly exciting feature of Silverlight is its ability to paint surfaces with video using a *VideoBrush*. This is a very straightforward process. First, you'll need a media element that loads the video. This media element should be hidden and should not accept mouse events. You achieve this by setting its opacity to 0 and by setting the *IsHitTestVisible* property to *false*. You'll also have to name the media element object using the *x:Name* property. Following is an example:

```
<MediaElement x:Name="vid" Source="balls.wmv" Opacity="0" IsHitTestVisible="False" />
```

Now the *VideoBrush* object can be applied to an object in the same manner as any other brush. You need to specify the brush source as the *MediaElement* (which is why it had to be named). You can also specify the *Stretch* property to further control the visual brush effect.

For example, here's a *TextBlock* containing text that has its *Foreground* color painted using a *VideoBrush*:

```
<TextBlock FontFamily="Verdana" FontSize="80"
    FontWeight="Bold" TextWrapping="Wrap"
    Text="Video">
  <TextBlock.Foreground>
    <VideoBrush SourceName="vid"/>
  </TextBlock.Foreground>
</TextBlock>
```

Silverlight will now render the text using a *VideoBrush*, and Figure 4-13 shows how this will display.

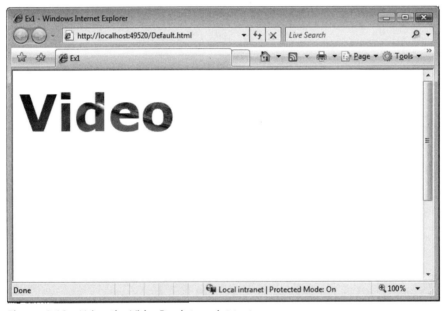

Figure 4-13   Using the VideoBrush to paint text.

Summary

This chapter provided you with an in-depth look at the *MediaElement* control and how it can be used to add video and audio media to your Silverlight application. You learned about the video formats and protocols that are supported and then discovered how to add the control to your Silverlight application. You saw how the different stretch modes of the media affect the way that your media is rendered, and how aspect ratio can be maintained. You learned how to place controls in front of or behind video media, making functionality such as subtitles or pop-up messages on video possible. You also saw how video can be transformed or clipped using XAML and then looked into the methods and properties that provide control and status of the playback of the video. These methods include user interactivity through playing, pausing, and stopping the video, as well as providing status feedback through buffering and download progress notification. In addition, you explored timelines and timeline markers and saw how easy these are to capture and process in Silverlight. Finally, you learned about the *VideoBrush* and how you can use this feature to paint surfaces with video.

If you've been reading this book in order, then you probably noticed that a lot of JavaScript programming was used in this chapter that was not part of the code in earlier chapters. You'll learn more about JavaScript programming in Chapter 5, which provides in-depth information about how to program Silverlight elements in JavaScript.

Chapter 5

Programming Silverlight with JavaScript

In this chapter, we'll take an in-depth look at programming the Silverlight object and the XAML it contains using JavaScript within the browser. We'll investigate how to host the Silverlight object in the browser, as well as the full property, method, and event model that the control supports. We'll also look at how to support loading and error events on the control, as well as how to handle parameterization and context for the control. You'll see how Silverlight provides a default error handler and how you can override this with your own error handlers. You'll delve into the *Downloader* object that is exposed by Silverlight, and how this can be used to dynamically add content to your application. Finally, we'll explore the programming model for the user interface (UI) elements that make up the XAML control model, and you will learn how you can use the methods and events that they expose from within the Java-Script programming model.

Hosting Silverlight in the Browser

You don't need any special software to be able to use and build Silverlight applications other than the Silverlight plug-in itself and the Silverlight.js file that manages downloading and installing the plug-in for clients that don't have it. You can use any software for building Web sites to build Silverlight sites, from Notepad to Eclipse to Expression Web or Expression Blend—it's really up to you.

This section presents a basic primer that will show you what you need to do to begin to use Silverlight. So far in this book, you've been using an Expression Blend or Visual Studio template to do the hard work for you, but now let's take a look at what it takes to get a simple Silverlight site up and running without any tools other than Windows Explorer and Notepad.

The first and most important file that you will need is the standard Silverlight.js file. This is available in the Silverlight Software Development Kit (SDK), which you can download from the Web site *http://www.microsoft.com/silverlight*.

Next, you'll need to create an HTML file that will reference this JavaScript file. You'll host the Silverlight control in this page. Here's an example:

```
<HTML>
   <HEAD>
      <script type="text/javascript" src="Silverlight.js" />
   </HEAD>
   <BODY>
   </BODY>
</HTML>
```

The Silverlight.js file contains methods called *createObject* and *createObjectEx* that you can use to instantiate Silverlight. The difference between these is that *createObjectEx* can use the JavaScript Object Notation (JSON) to serialize the parameters.

These functions take a set of parameters that are used to instantiate the control. The parameters are described in Table 5-1.

Table 5-1   Parameters for *createObject* and *createObjectEx*

Parameter Name	Description
source	This sets the source for the XAML code that the control renders. It can be a file reference (i.e.,"source.xaml"), a URI (i.e., *http://server/ generatexaml.aspx*) ,or a reference to inline XAML contained within a DIV (i.e., *#xamlcontent* for a DIV named *xamlcontent*).
parentElement	This is the name of the DIV that contains the Silverlight control on your HTML page.
ID	This is the unique ID that you assign to an instance of the Silverlight control.
width	This sets the width of the control in pixels or by percentage.
height	This sets the height of the control in pixels or by percentage.
background	This determines the background color of the control. See the section titled *"SolidColorBrush"* in Chapter 2, "Silverlight and XAML," for more details on how to set colors. You can use an ARGB value, such as #FFAA7700, or a named color, such as *Black*.
framerate	This sets the maximum frame rate to allow for animation. It defaults to 24.
isWindowless	This is set to *true* or *false* and defaults to *false*. When it is set *true*, the Silverlight content is rendered behind the HTML content, so that HTML content can be written on top of it.
enableHtmlAccess	This determines if the content that is hosted in the Silverlight control is accessible from the browser DOM. It defaults to *true*.
inplaceInstallPrompt	Silverlight has two modes of installation. An *inplace* install involves accepting the software license and downloading the control directly without leaving the site hosting it. An *indirect* install involves having the user transfer to the Microsoft download site for Silverlight. From there they accept the license and download the control. You control which method will be presented to the user with this property. Setting the property to *true* allows the user direct *inplace* installation; a *false* setting leads to the *indirect* installation.
version	This determines the minimum version of Silverlight to support.

Table 5-1   Parameters for *createObject* and *createObjectEx*

Parameter Name	Description
onLoad	This specifies the function to run when the control is loaded.
onError	This specifies the function to run when the control hits an error.
onFullScreenChange	This event is fired when the *FullScreen* property of the Silverlight control changes.
onResize	This event is fired when the *ActualWidth* or *ActualHeight* property of the Silverlight control changes.
initParams	This specifies a user-definable set of parameters to load into the control. For more details on this, see the section titled "Handling Parameters" later in this chapter.
userContext	This specifies a unique identifier that can be passed as a parameter to the *onLoad* event handler function. You'll see more of this in the "Responding to Page Load Events" section later in this chapter.

Please note that the *width, height, background, framerate, iswindowless, enableHtmlAccess, version,* and *inplaceInstallPrompt* properties are handled within a properties array when creating an instance of the control, and the *onLoad* and *onError* are handled within the events array.

Following is an example:

```
Silverlight.createObject(
    "Scene.xaml",
    document.getElementById("SilverlightControlHost"),
    "mySilverlightControl",
    {
        width:'300',
        height:'300',
        inplaceInstallPrompt:false,
        background:'#D6D6D6',
        isWindowless:'false',
        framerate:'24',
        version:'1.0'
    },
    {
        onError:null,
        onLoad:null
    },
    null);
```

This call is typically hosted in an external file, and the de facto standard for this file is named createSilverlight.js. You'll need a reference to this in your HTML to be able to access the function.

So, let's now return to our HTML page and set it up so that it can handle this Silverlight control. You see that when the Silverlight component was named, it was expecting a parent DIV called *SilverlightControlHost* to host it. This is achieved using the *ID* property of the DIV. Here's the full HTML code:

```
<html>
<head>
   <script type="text/javascript" src="Silverlight.js"></script>
   <script type="text/javascript" src="createSilverlight.js"></script>
</head>

<body>
   <div id="SilverlightControlHost">
      <script type="text/javascript">
         createSilverlight();
      </script>
   </div>
</body>
</html>
```

Finally, you'll need the XAML source for your Silverlight control. This sample calls for a XAML file called Scene.xaml.

Following is a simple XAML file that contains a "Hello, World!" *TextBlock*:

```
<Canvas xmlns="http://schemas.microsoft.com/client/2007"
        xmlns:x="http://schemas.microsoft.com/winfx/2006/xaml">
  <TextBlock>Hello, World!</TextBlock>
</Canvas>
```

And that's everything that you need to get a Silverlight application set up and ready to go. As you add more functionality to your application, your code will become more complex, but these four files—the HTML host, the XAML file, createSilverlight.js, and Silverlight.js—are common to every project.

Responding to Page Load Events

You specify a JavaScript event handler to manage page load events using the *onLoad* parameter introduced in Table 5-1. This fires after the XAML content within the Silverlight control has completely loaded. Note that if you have defined a loaded event on any XAML UI element, those events will fire before the Silverlight control's *onLoad* event does. In addition to this, the control has a read-only *IsLoaded* property that is set immediately before the *onLoad* event fires.

When using an *onLoad* event handler, your JavaScript function should take three parameters: The first is a reference to the control, the second is the user context, and the third is a reference to the root element of the XAML. Following is an example:

```
function handleLoad(control, userContext, rootElement)
{
    ...
}
```

Handling Parameters

When you call the *createObject* function to instantiate Silverlight, you can pass parameters to it using the *initParams* property. This property is a string value, so, if you have multiple values, you can encode them into a comma separated string which is easily sliced in JavaScript. Following is an example of setting up the Silverlight control that has three parameters:

```
function createSilverlight()
{
    Silverlight.createObject(
        "Scene.xaml",
        document.getElementById("SilverlightControlHost"),
        "mySilverlightControl",
        {
            width:'300',
            height:'300',
            inplaceInstallPrompt:false,
            background:'#D6D6D6',
            isWindowless:'false',
            framerate:'24',
            version:'1.0'
        },
        {
            onError:null,
            onLoad:handleLoad
        },
        "p1, p2, p3", // Parameter List
        null);
}
```

Here the parameters *p1*, *p2*, and *p3* are encoded into a comma-separated string. JavaScript has a string *split* method that allows you to split a comma-separated string into an array of values.

Following is an example of an *onLoad* event handler that uses this method to split the parameter list into an array of strings and to display each one in an alert box.

```
function handleLoad(control, userContext, rootElement)
{
    var params = control.initParams.split(",");
    for (var i = 0; i< params.length; i++)
    {
        alert(params[i]);
    }
}
```

User Context

An additional parameter that can be passed to the Silverlight control is the context parameter. This will be included directly in the *onLoad* event as the second parameter, typically named *userContext*. It behaves exactly the same as the previous parameters you've seen, in that it is a property value that can be queried after the control has rendered. Typically, user context is not used for control parameters, however. It is instead used as a reference variable to distinguish different controls, though there is nothing to prevent you from using it to parameterize your control.

Following is an example of a page that hosts two Silverlight controls. Note that the name and context variables are set in this host page and then referenced within the JavaScript that creates the Silverlight control:

```html
<html>
<head>
    <script type="text/javascript" src="Silverlight.js"></script>
    <script type="text/javascript" src="createSilverlight.js"></script>
    <script type="text/javascript">
        function handleLoad(control, userContext, rootElement)
        {
            alert(userContext);
        }
    </script>
</head>

<body>
    <div id="firstControl">
        <script type="text/javascript">
            var parentElement = document.getElementById("firstControl");
            var name = "agc1";
            var context = "the first control";
            createSilverlight();
        </script>
    </div>
    <div id="secondControl">
        <script type="text/javascript">
            var parentElement = document.getElementById("secondControl");
            var name = "agc2";
            var context = "the second control";
            createSilverlight();
        </script>
    </div>
</body>
</html>
```

Here you can see two DIV elements, called *firstControl* and *secondControl*. They set up the *parentElement*, *name*, and *context* values before calling a modified version of *createSilverlight*:

```javascript
function createSilverlight()
{
    Silverlight.createObject(
        "Scene.xaml",
        parentElement,
        name,
        {
            width:'300',
            height:'300',
            inplaceInstallPrompt:false,
```

```
            background:'#D6D6D6',
            isWindowless:'false',
            framerate:'24',
            version:'1.0'
        },
        {
            onError:null,
            onLoad:handleLoad
        },
        "p1, p2, p3", // Parameter List
        context);
    }
```

This takes the *parentElement, name,* and *context* values that were set up within the HTML page that you saw earlier, demonstrating that the same *createSilverlight* function can be spread across multiple controls.

The HTML page contains the *onLoad* event handler, which you can see here:

```
<script type="text/javascript">
    function handleLoad(control, userContext, rootElement)
    {
        alert(userContext);
    }
</script>
```

This takes the *userContext* parameter and displays the context value in an alert box. You can see how this appears on screen in Figure 5-1, where the HTML page is displaying the context for the first control.

Responding to Page Error Events

Silverlight provides several methods for error handling, depending on the type of error. Errors are raised when the XAML parser hits a problem, loading isn't completed properly, run-time errors are encountered, and when event handlers defined in the XAML document do not have a JavaScript function associated with them.

When initializing a control using the *onError* event handler, you specify a JavaScript function that will be called when an error occurs. However, if you do not specify one (or if you specify it as *null*), the default JavaScript event handler will fire.

Figure 5-1   Displaying control context.

The Default Event Handler

The JavaScript default event handler will display an error message alert box that contains basic details about the Silverlight error, including the error code and type as well as a message defining the specific problem and the method name that was called.

Following is an example of a badly formed XAML document, in which the closing tag of the *TextBlock* element is misnamed *</TextBlok>*:

```
<Canvas xmlns="http://schemas.microsoft.com/client/2007"
        xmlns:x="http://schemas.microsoft.com/winfx/2006/xaml">
  <TextBlock>Hello, World!</TextBlok>
</Canvas>
```

If the error handler is set to *null*, then the default error handler will fire and display the default Silverlight error message, as shown in Figure 5-2.

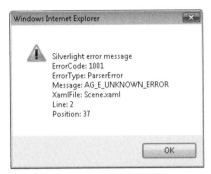

Figure 5-2   The default error message.

Using Your Own Error Handler

You can use your own error handler by setting the *onError* property of the Silverlight control to a custom event handler function. Your error handler function will need to take two parameters: the sender object and the event arguments that define the specifics of the error that occurred.

There are three types of event argument that you can receive. The first is the basic *ErrorEventArgs* object that contains the error message type and code. The *errorType* property defines the type of error as a string containing *RuntimeError* or *ParserError*. Based on this information, you can use one of the two associated derived error types.

When processing a parsing error in XAML, the *ParserErrorEventArgs* is available. This contains a number of properties:

- The *charposition* property contains the character position where the error occurred.
- The *linenumber* property contains the line where the error occurred.
- The *xamlFile* identifies the file in which the error occurred.
- The *xmlAttribute* identifies the xml attribute in which the error occurred.
- The *xmlElement* defines the element in which the error occurred.

Run-time errors are defined in the *RuntimeErrorEventArgs* object. This object also contains a number of properties:

- The *charPosition* property identifies the character position where the error occurred.
- The *lineNumber* property identifies the line in which the error occurred.
- The *methodName* identifies the method associated with the error.

In the previous section, you saw a parsing error as trapped by the default error handler. Here's how you could capture the same error with your own error handler. First, you create the *createSilverlight()* method that sets up the error handler:

```
function createSilverlight()
{
    Silverlight.createObject(
        "Scene.xaml",
        document.getElementById("firstControl"),
        "agc1",
        {
            width:'300',
            height:'300',
            inplaceInstallPrompt:false,
            background:'#D6D6D6',
            isWindowless:'false',
            framerate:'24',
            version:'1.0'
        },
        {
            onError:handleError,
            onLoad:null
        },
        null);
}
```

Following is the HTML file that calls this revised Silverlight creation method and contains the *handleError* function that was defined as the error handler using the *onError* attribute:

```
<html>
<head>
    <script type="text/javascript" src="Silverlight.js"></script>
    <script type="text/javascript" src="createSilverlight.js"></script>
    <script type="text/javascript">
        function handleError(sender, errorArguments)
        {
            var strError = "Error Details: \n";
            strError+= "Type: " + errorArguments.errorType + "\n";
            strError+= "Message: " + errorArguments.errorMessage + "\n";
            strError+= "Code: " + errorArguments.errorCode + "\n";
            // We know (in this case) that its a parser error.
            // For a more generic error handler
            // you should trap on error type before calling
            // properties on a specific argument type.
            strError+= "Xaml File: " + errorArguments.xamlFile + "\n";
            strError+= "Xaml Element: " + errorArguments.xmlElement + "\n";
            strError+= "Xaml Attribute: " + errorArguments.xmlAttribute + "\n";
            strError+= "Line: " + errorArguments.lineNumber + "\n";
            strError+= "Position: " + errorArguments.charPosition + "\n";
            alert(strError);
        }
    </script>
</head>
```

```
<body>
   <div id="firstControl">
      <script type="text/javascript">
         createSilverlight();
      </script>
   </div>
</body>
</html>
```

When this is executed and the error is tripped, the alert box will display the contents of the error. Figure 5-3 shows an example of a customized alert box.

Figure 5-3   Using your own event handler.

Silverlight Control Properties

The Silverlight control has a number of properties, some of which were discussed in the section titled "Hosting Silverlight in the Browser." In addition to being able to set them when you initialize the control, you can also set the controls properties using script. The control splits properties into three types: direct, content, and settings properties. *Direct* properties are properties of the control itself that are accessible using the *control.propertyname* syntax. *Content* properties and *settings* properties are accessed using the *control.content.propertyname* and *control.settings.propertyname* syntax respectively.

Direct Properties

Following are the direct properties that are supported:

- **initParams**   The initialization parameters that are passed to the control are stored in this property. It can only be set as part of the control initialization.

- **isLoaded**   This property is *true* after the control is loaded; otherwise it is *false*. It is read-only.

- **source**   This is the XAML content that you want to render. It can be a reference to a file, a URI to a service that generates XAML, or, when prefixed with a # character, it is a DIV containing XAML code in a script block.

Content Properties

When accessing content properties, you use the *control.content.propertyname* syntax. For example, if you want to access the *actualHeight* property, you use the *control.content.actualHeight* syntax. The following content properties are available:

- **actualHeight**   This returns the height of the rendering area of the Silverlight control in pixels. The value returned depends on a number of different criteria. First, it depends on how the height of the control was initially set. Recall that it can be a percentage or an absolute pixel value. In the case of the former, the *actualHeight* property is the current height of the control, but if the user changes the browser dimensions, this will change. If the height was set using an absolute pixel value, this will be returned. When the control is used in full screen mode, this will return the current vertical resolution of the display.

- **actualWidth**   This returns the width of the display. The value returned depends on a number of criteria and is similar to the *actualHeight* parameter.

- **fullScreen**   This switches the Silverlight control display between embedded and full screen mode. It defaults to *false*, which is the embedded mode. When set to *true*, Silverlight will render to the full screen.

Settings Properties

The control also contains a number of properties that are defined as settings properties, where they are accessed using the *control.settings.propertyname* syntax:

- **background**   This sets the background color of the Silverlight control. It can take several different formats, including a named color (such as Black), 8Bit Red/Green/Blue (RGB) values with or without alpha, and 16Bit RGB values with or without alpha.

- **enableFrameRateCounter**   When set to *true*, Silverlight will render the current frame rate (in frames per second) in the browser's status bar. It defaults to *false*.

- *enableHtmlAccess*   When set to *true*, this will allow the XAML content to be accessible from the browser DOM. The default value is *true*.

- *enableRedrawRegions*   When set to *true*, this shows the areas of the plug-in that are being redrawn upon each frame. It's a useful tool to help you optimize your application. The default value is *false*.

- *maxFrameRate*   This specifies the maximum frame rate to render it. It defaults to 24 and has an absolute maximum of 64.

- *version*   This reports the version of the Silverlight control that is presently being used. It is a string containing up to four integers, separated by dots, which contain the major, minor, build, and revision number, though only the first two values (major and minor version number) are required.

- *windowless*   This determines whether the property is displayed as a windowless or windowed control. When set to *true*, it is windowless, meaning the Silverlight content is effectively rendered "behind" the HTML content on the page.

Silverlight Control Methods

The Silverlight control has a number of methods that you can use to control its behavior and function. Similar to Silverlight property groups, the Silverlight methods are grouped into "families" of methods. At present, one direct and three content methods are supported. You'll see which is which in the following sections, including samples showing their syntax and how to access them.

The *createFromXaml* Method

The *createFromXaml* method is a Silverlight content method that allows you to define XAML content to dynamically add to your Silverlight control. It takes two parameters. The first is a string containing the XAML that you want to use, and the other is the *namescope* parameter that, when *true* (it defaults to *false*), will create unique *x:Name* references within the provided XAML that will not conflict with any existing XAML element names.

There is a constraint around the XAML that you can add using *createFromXaml*. The XAML you add has to have a single root node. So, if you have a number of elements to add, make sure that they are all contained within a single containing *Canvas* element.

Additionally, *createFromXaml* does not add the XAML to the Silverlight control until it has been added to the children of one of the *Canvas* elements within the control. So, when you call *createFromXaml*, you get a reference to the node returned, and this reference is then used to add the node into the render tree. Following is an example:

```
function handleLoad(control, userContext, sender)
{
    var xamlFragment = '<TextBlock Canvas.Top="60" Text="A new TextBlock" />';
    textBlock = control.content.createFromXaml(xamlFragment);
    sender.children.add(textBlock);
}
```

Here the XAML code for a text block control is created, containing the text "A new TextBlock". This is then used to create an XAML node within the control content, and after it is complete, Silverlight will return a reference to the text block. This reference is then added to the Silverlight control's render tree and is used to render the context of the text block.

The *createFromXamlDownloader* Method

The *createFromXamlDownloader* method is a content method used in conjunction with a *Downloader* object, which you will learn about later in this chapter. It takes two parameters. The first parameter is a reference to the *Downloader* object that downloads the XAML code, or a package containing the XAML code. The second parameter is the name of the specific part of the download content package to use. If this is a .zip file, then you specify the name of the file within the .zip file that contains the XAML code you want to use. When the downloaded content is not in a .zip package, then this parameter should be set to an empty string.

The *createObject* method

The *createObject* method is a direct method designed to allow you to create a disposable object for a specific function. In Silverlight 1.0, the only object that is supported is the *Downloader* object. We'll cover this in greater detail later in this chapter.

The *findName* method

This content method allows you to search for a node within your XAML code based on its *x:Name* attribute. If *findName* finds a node with the provided name, it returns a reference to it; otherwise it returns *null*.

The *Downloader* Object

The Silverlight control provides an object that allows you to download additional elements using asynchronous downloading functionality. This allows you to download individual assets, or assets that are packaged in a .zip file.

Downloader Object Properties

The *Downloader* object supports the following properties:

- **downloadProgress** This property provides a normalized value (between 0 and 1) representing the percentage progress of the content downloaded, where 1 is equal to 100 percent complete.

- *status*   This property gets the HTTP status code for the current status of the downloading process. It returns a standard HTTP status code, for example "404" for "Not Found" or "200" for "OK".

- *statusText*   This property gets the HTTP status text for the current status of the downloading process. This corresponds to the status code for the *status* property. For a successful request, the *status* will be "200," and the *statusText* will be "OK." For more information about HTTP status codes, check out the standard HTTP codes provided by W3C (*http://www.w3.org/Protocols/rfc2616/rfc2616-sec10.html*).

- *uri*   This property contains the URI of the object that the downloader is presently accessing.

Downloader Object Methods

The *Downloader* object supports the following methods:

- *abort*   This cancels the current download and resets all properties to their default state.

- *getResponseText*   This returns a string representation of the downloaded data. It takes an optional parameter that is used to name the contents of the file name within a downloaded package.

- *open*   This initializes the download session. It takes three parameters. The first is the verb for the action. The set of HTTP verbs is documented by the W3C; however, only the *GET* verb is supported in Silverlight 1.0. The second parameter is the URI for the resource that is to be downloaded. The optional third parameter determines if the download is synchronous or asynchronous. It defaults to *true* (for asynchronous download).

- *send*   This executes the download request that was initialized with the *Open* command.

Downloader Object Events

The *Downloader* object supports the following events:

- *completed*   This event will fire when the download is complete. It takes two parameters. The first is the object that raised the event (in this case, the downloader control itself), and the second is a set of event arguments (*eventArgs*). In Silverlight 1.0, the *eventArgs* parameter is always *null*.

- *downloadProgressChanged*   This event will fire while content is being downloaded. It fires every time the progress (which is a value between 0 and 1) changes by 0.05 (5 percent) or more, as well as when it reaches 1.0 (100 percent). When it reaches 1.0, the *completed* event will also fire.

Using the *Downloader* Object

You create a *Downloader* object using the *createObject* method provided by the Silverlight control. Here's an example:

```
<script type="text/javascript">
    function handleLoad(control, userContext, sender)
    {
        var downloader = control.createObject("downloader");
    }
</script>
```

The next step is to initialize the download session by using the *Downloader* object's *open* method to declare the URI of the file, and then to call the *send* method to kick off the download. Following is an example that will download a movie file called *movie.wmv*:

```
function handleLoad(control, userContext, sender)
{
    var downloader = control.createObject("downloader");
    downloader.open("GET","movie.wmv",true);
    downloader.send();
}
```

In order to trap the download progress and completion, you'll need to wire the appropriate event handlers. Following is the same function, updated accordingly:

```
function handleLoad(control, userContext, sender)
{
    var downloader = control.createObject("downloader");
    downloader.addEventListener("downloadProgressChanged","handleDLProgress");
    downloader.addEventListener("completed","handleDLComplete");
    downloader.open("GET","movie.wmv",true);
    downloader.send();
}
```

Now you can implement these event handlers. In this example, the *DownloadProgressChanged* event is wired to a JavaScript function called *handleDLProgress,* and the *Completed* event is wired to the *handleDLComplete* JavaScript function. You can see these functions here:

```
function handleDLProgress(sender, args)
{
    var ctrl = sender.getHost();
    var t1 = ctrl.content.findName("txt1");
    var v = sender.downloadProgress * 100;
    t1.Text = v + "%";
}

function handleDLComplete(sender, args)
{
    alert("Download complete");
}
```

Programming UI Elements

XAML provides a number of visual elements for creating your user interfaces. These are listed in detail in Chapter 2, where their properties are discussed. The set of UI elements includes *Canvas, Ellipse, Glyphs, Image, Line, MediaElement, Path, Polygon, Polyline, Rectangle, Run, Shape,* and *TextBlock.*

Each of these elements supports a rich set of methods and events, and these will be listed and discussed in the next several sections.

UI Element Methods

UI elements provide functions that can be called from JavaScript to allow you to manipulate them to create rich application interaction. These methods are common to all of the UI elements.

The *AddEventListener* and *RemoveEventListener* Methods

The *AddEventListener* method is used to add an event listener at run time to the UI element. This is useful for separating design and development—the developer doesn't add anything directly to the XAML that the designer produces. Instead, the developer adds event handling code to a JavaScript file (or block). UI element events you might handle are discussed later in this chapter.

Note   When using the *AddEventListener* method, be sure to define the name of the event using a lowercase letter for the first character. For example, if you are defining an event handler for the *MouseLeftButtonDown* event using the *addEventListener* method, you declare it using the string "mouseLeftButtonDown".

Following is an example that shows you how to add an event listener at run time. This example adds an event handler that traps the mouse click and specifies that the event should be handled by a JavaScript function called *handleMouse.* This function, like most event handlers, takes two parameters, a sender and event arguments. Because it is a mouse event, it takes an instance of *MouseEventArgs,* which allows us to get the x- and y-coordinates of the mouse at the time of the event:

```
<script type="text/javascript">
    function handleLoad(control, userContext, sender)
    {
        sender.addEventListener("mouseLeftButtonDown",handleMouse);
    }
    function handleMouse(sender, mouseEventArgs)
    {
        alert(mouseEventArgs.getPosition(null).x + ":"
            + mouseEventArgs.getPosition(null).y);
```

```
    }
</script>
```

You can destroy the connection at run time using the *RemoveEventListener* method with the same syntax.

The *findName* Method

This method is used to search through the child elements of a particular element to find a named object. It will return a reference to the specified object if it exists; otherwise it will return *null*. For example, take a look at this XAML code:

```
<Canvas xmlns="http://schemas.microsoft.com/client/2007"
        xmlns:x="http://schemas.microsoft.com/winfx/2006/xaml"
        Height="400" Width="400">
  <TextBlock Canvas.Top="0" x:Name="txt1" Text="TextBlock1" />
  <TextBlock Canvas.Top="20" x:Name="txt2" Text="TextBlock2" />
  <TextBlock Canvas.Top="40" x:Name="txt3" Text="TextBlock3" />
</Canvas>
```

This code defines three text blocks called *txt1*, *txt2*, and *txt3* using the *x:Name* property. You can now use the *findName* method to find a named node, obtain a reference to it, and then edit it using that reference. In this case, it is done within the *handleLoad* event handler.

```
<script type="text/javascript">
    function handleLoad(control, userContext, sender)
    {
        var t1 = sender.findName("txt1");
        t1.Text = "TextBlock1 has changed";
    }
</script>
```

Accessing the Control with the *GetHost* Method

UI elements provide a *GetHost* method that can be used to get a handle to the containing Silverlight control. This is useful when you want to use an event handler on one control to access a different control.

An example of this can be seen in the event handler for the download progress of a *Downloader* object. In this case, the function doesn't have direct access to the Silverlight control, but in order to manipulate the properties of another element, the UI element event handler needs a reference to that element (in this example, a reference to the Silverlight control). The UI element event handler can do this by getting a reference to the control using *getHost*, and then from that reference it can find the other element.

```
function handleDLProgress(sender, args)
{
    var ctrl = sender.getHost();
    var t1 = ctrl.content.findName("txt1");
    var v = sender.downloadProgress * 100;
```

```
    t1.Text = v + "%";
}
```

Accessing a Parent Element with the *getParent* Method

You may have cases in which you want to access a UI element's parent. It is inefficient to get a reference to the Silverlight control and then to use *findName* to get the parent, so the *getParent* method is available. It will return a reference to the parent upon success; otherwise it will return *null*.

Using the *GetValue* and *SetValue* Methods

You can always access properties with the traditional dot syntax, *object.propertyname*, but an alternative methodology, using the *GetValue* method, exists to support attached properties. So, for example, if you want to access the *Canvas.Top* property, you cannot do it with *object.Canvas.Top*. You must use the *object.GetValue("Canvas.Top")* syntax. *GetValue* can also be used to access nonattached properties, even though in that case the dot notation is equivalent.

In a similar way, you can use the *SetValue* method to set a property value for either a simple or attached property. This method takes two parameters. The first is the name of the property, and the second is the value to assign. Following is an example:

```
var t1 = ctrl.content.findName("txt1");
t1.setValue("Canvas.Top",20);
```

Using *SetFontSource*

The *TextBlock* element supports an additional method, *SetFontSource*, that adds font files to the object's collection of fonts that it can use. So, if you want to use a new font to render the text—for example, if you need to support a foreign character set (such as a font used for an East Asian language), then you can download the font with a *Downloader* object and use the *Set-FontSource* method, passing it the *Downloader* and the *TextBlock* will use that font. To use this method, you must have the rights to distribute the font (or a subset thereof).

Following is an example using the *SetFontSource* method. In this case, I have an XAML document that was defined using Expression Blend and that uses some Chinese text:

```
<Canvas
  xmlns="http://schemas.microsoft.com/client/2007"
  xmlns:x="http://schemas.microsoft.com/winfx/2006/xaml"
  Width="640" Height="480" Background="White">
   <TextBlock x:Name="myTextBlock" Width="152" Height="64"
     Canvas.Left="184" Canvas.Top="56" Text="你好，你好吗?"
     TextWrapping="Wrap" MouseLeftButtonDown="handleIt" />
</Canvas>
```

When this is rendered, the default Silverlight font set will not recognize the Chinese characters and will print them as *unprintable* character blocks (typically small squares). However, you can use a *Downloader* object to download a font that *does* support Chinese text. The previous XAML code defines a *MouseLeftButtonDown* event handler function called *handleIt*. You can see that function here:

```
// Event handler for initializing and executing a font file download request.
function handleIt(sender, eventArgs)
{
    // Retrieve a reference to the control.
    var control = sender.getHost();
    // Create a Downloader object.
    var downloader = control.createObject("downloader");
    // Add Completed event.
    downloader.addEventListener("Completed", "onCompleted");
    // Initialize the Downloader request.
    downloader.open("GET", "SIMHEI.TTF", true);
    // Execute the Downloader request.
    downloader.send();
}
```

This creates a download object that downloads the font and defines an event handler *onCompleted* that will handle the *Completed* event that fires when the download is complete. This event will then set the font source for the *TextBlock* to the supporting font, and then Silverlight will render the Chinese characters using the new font source.

```
// Event handler for the Completed event.
function onCompleted(sender, eventArgs)
{
    // Retrieve the TextBlock object.
    var myTextBlock = sender.findName("myTextBlock");

    // Add the font files in the downloaded object
    // to the TextBlock's type face collection.
    myTextBlock.setFontSource(sender);

    // Set the FontFamily property to the friendly name of the font.
    myTextBlock.fontFamily = "Simhei";
}
```

UI Element Events

UI elements support a number of events that may be wired to JavaScript functions either by using the *AddEventListener* methodology to add them at run time, or by using the appropriate XAML attribute to add them at design time. For example, if you want to wire a control's *MouseLeftButtonDown* event using JavaScript, you do it with the *AddEventListener* method:

```
t1.addEventListener("MouseLeftButtonDown", handleMouseDown);
```

To wire the event in XAML, you can use the attribute that has the same name as the desired event (such as "MouseLeftButtonDown"). Following is an example:

```
<TextBlock Canvas.Top="0" x:Name="txt1" Text="Status"
MouseLeftButtonDown="handleMouseDown"/>
```

The events that are supported on the UI element are as follows:

- **GotFocus**   This is fired when the element receives mouse focus.

- **KeyDown**   Occurs on an element when it has focus and a key is pressed. The event handler takes two attributes. The first of these is the *sender*, representing a reference to the object that raised the event. The second is a *KeyEventArgs* object. This has a number of properties of its own. The first is *key*, which is an integer value that represents the key that was pressed. It is not operating-system specific, and specific details about how this maps to actual keys can be found in the Silverlight SDK. Another property is the *platformKeyCode*, which *is* operating-system specific. In addition to the actual key, the Boolean properties *shift* and *ctrl* are exposed. These indicate whether or not the Shift and Ctrl keys are pressed.

- **KeyUp**   This occurs on an element when it has focus and the key is released. It provides for the same two attributes as the *KeyDown* event.

- **Loaded**   This fires when the Silverlight content is loaded into the host Silverlight control and parsed, but before it is rendered.

- **LostFocus**   This is the opposite of the *GotFocus* event; it fires when the object loses focus.

- **MouseEnter**   This fires when the mouse enters the bounding area of the object.

- **MouseLeave**   This is the opposite of *MouseEnter* event; it fires when the mouse leaves the area of the bounding object.

- **MouseLeftButtonDown**   This occurs when the user presses the left mouse button over the UI element.

- **MouseLeftButtonUp**   This occurs when the left mouse button is released.

- **MouseMove**   This occurs when the cursor moves over the UI element.

Implementing Drag and Drop

You can use the mouse event handlers and Silverlight's *CaptureMouse* and *ReleaseMouseCapture* methods to implement drag and drop in Silverlight.

First of all, let's take a look at a XAML document containing several shapes that may be dragged and dropped around the canvas. These shapes wire their mouse event handlers (*MouseLeftButtonDown*, *MouseLeftButtonUp* and *MouseMove*) to the *onMouseDown*, *onMouseUp*, and *onMouseMove* functions respectively.

```
<Canvas xmlns="http://schemas.microsoft.com/client/2007"
        xmlns:x="http://schemas.microsoft.com/winfx/2006/xaml"
        Height="400" Width="400">
<Ellipse Canvas.Top="0" Height="10" Width="10" Fill="Black"
        MouseLeftButtonDown="onMouseDown"
        MouseLeftButtonUp="onMouseUp"
        MouseMove="onMouseMove" />
<Ellipse Canvas.Top="20" Height="10" Width="10" Fill="Black"
        MouseLeftButtonDown="onMouseDown"
        MouseLeftButtonUp="onMouseUp"
        MouseMove="onMouseMove"/>
<Ellipse Canvas.Top="40" Height="10" Width="10" Fill="Black"
        MouseLeftButtonDown="onMouseDown"
        MouseLeftButtonUp="onMouseUp"
        MouseMove="onMouseMove"/>
<Ellipse Canvas.Top="60" Height="10" Width="10" Fill="Black"
        MouseLeftButtonDown="onMouseDown"
        MouseLeftButtonUp="onMouseUp"
        MouseMove="onMouseMove"/>
</Canvas>
```

Now let's take a look at each of the event handler functions. First, let's examine the mouse down event handler. When dragging, you want that control to "own" the mouse events, so you use the *captureMouse* method. You'll also want to remember the starting points for the dragging, so these will be recorded by the event handler. Finally, you'll flag that the mouse is down using a Boolean variable *isMouseDown*.

```
var beginX;
var beginY;
var isMouseDown = false;
function onMouseDown(sender, mouseEventArgs)
{
    beginX = mouseEventArgs.getPosition(null).x;
    beginY = mouseEventArgs.getPosition(null).y;
    isMouseDown = true;
    sender.captureMouse();
}
```

Now, in a drag-and-drop operation, you want to move the item with the mouse. So, when the *MouseMove* event fires, you will record the current mouse coordinates and use them to figure out where the item should be moved as well.

The *mouseEventArgs* allow us to retrieve the current x- and y-coordinates of the mouse, and since the *Ellipse* object that is being dragged in the example is the *sender*, you can set its left and top properties by adding the delta on the x- and y-coordinates to their respective initial values.

Also note that *onMouseMove* will fire whether you are dragging or not, so we use the *isMouseDown* to check if we are currently dragging. (Remember, it was set in the previous *MouseDown* event handler.)

```
function onMouseMove(sender, mouseEventArgs)
{
  if (isMouseDown == true)
    {
        var currX = mouseEventArgs.getPosition(null).x;
        var currY = mouseEventArgs.getPosition(null).y;
        sender["Canvas.Left"] += currX - beginX;
        sender["Canvas.Top"] += currY - beginY;
        beginX = currX;
        beginY = currY;
    }
}
```

Finally, when the mouse button is released, you will release the mouse capture and reset *isMouseDown*. The ellipses will stay in their new positions.

```
function onMouseUp(sender, mouseEventArgs)
{
    isMouseDown = false;
    sender.releaseMouseCapture();
}
```

Figure 5-4 shows the four ellipses with drag and drop enabled, and Figure 5-5 shows the position of the ellipses after the drag-and-drop operation has been completed.

Figure 5-4   Four ellipses with drag and drop enabled.

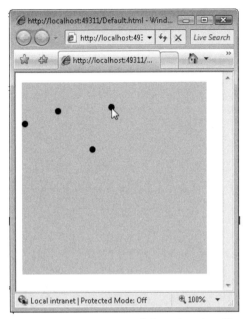

Figure 5-5 Dragging and dropping the ellipses.

Summary

In this chapter, you looked at the Silverlight object model and how it can be programmed using JavaScript. You learned how the Silverlight control is hosted within the browser, including how to initialize it, and how to set up its initial state using its property model. You saw how it can be customized with context and custom parameters, as well as the full property, method, and event model that it supports. In addition, you learned how to implement a custom error handler on the control, as well as how to use the basic default error handler.

You discovered how you can add external content to your control using the *Downloader* object and how to trap the events that it exposes to provide feedback as to download progress. You were introduced to the UI elements that XAML offers and learned about the methods, events, and properties that they expose and how you can program them.

In the next chapter, you'll look at how Silverlight supports ink and find out how the Tablet PC, the Touch Screen PC, and other interactive user interface types may be supported by your Web applications using Silverlight.

Chapter 6

Using Silverlight with Ink

As you've seen so far in this book, Silverlight empowers the design of the next generation of Web applications by providing tools that allow you to add rich video, audio, vector graphics, animation, and other enhancements that improve the user's experience. Ink annotation—the creation of handwriting or drawing content using a device designed for this purpose—is another great way to make applications even more interactive and personal, and Silverlight's support for Ink-based programming brings this functionality to the Web. In this chapter, we'll investigate how Ink annotation is supported in Silverlight 1.0.

There are several different types of device that can be used for Ink-based applications:

- **Pen Input**   Computers that support pen digitizers are typically Tablet PCs, but they can also be desktop computers that support external digitizers. These can take advantage of the pen input in Silverlight. They create *Ink* that can be integrated into Silverlight Web pages so that handwriting, drawing, annotation, and other input formats can be supported on the Web.

- **Touch Input**   Touch screens are very common in kiosk environments or other places where a stylus or keyboard would be unwieldy or unnecessary. Silverlight with Ink annotation supports touch screens, allowing rich Internet applications with touch-based interactivity.

- **Mouse Input**   The mouse can be used to provide digitized, penlike input similar to a Tablet PC pen. However, this Ink input will have a lower resolution than if you used a true Tablet PC pen.

An Example of Ink Annotation in Silverlight

Silverlight.net provides a great example of an application that supports Ink annotation. It is the page-turner application hosted at *http://silverlight.net/samples/1.0/Page-Turn/ default.html*. You can see it in Figure 6-1.

Figure 6-1 The Silverlight PageTurn sample.

This application demonstrates how you can download a source and browse through images and other assets using an application that mimics turning the pages of a book. It is enhanced with Ink, which allows you to annotate the images—and the annotations you add remain associated with the image. You can see an example of an annotated page in Figure 6-2.

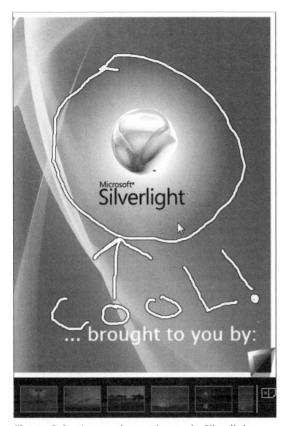

Figure 6-2 Annotating an image in Silverlight.

Silverlight Ink Classes

Support for Ink in Silverlight is very straightforward. Every time you drag the input device across the screen, you generate one or more *StylusPoint* objects. These are collected into a *StylusPointCollection*, which forms the basis of a *Stroke*. The strokes are collected into a *StrokeCollection*, which makes up the list of graphics that are used to create the Ink that the Ink Presenter renders. So, if you consider Figure 6-2, the letter "C" in *Cool* is a stroke that is made up of a number of points collected into its stroke collection. Each letter "o," the letter "l," the line and dot in the exclamation point, and the lines that make up the arrow and the circle are all strokes. Each of these strokes is a member of the Ink Presenter's *StrokeCollection*, and each of them is made up of *StylusPoint*s held in the relevant stroke's *StylusPointCollection*. Each of these types provides an object-oriented interface with properties and methods that allow them to be programmable.

The *StrokeCollection* Type

The *InkPresenter* object contains the *Strokes* property, which is an instance of *StrokeCollection*. This collection, in turn, contains all the metadata that is required to represent the user's Ink input.

StrokeCollection Properties

In Silverlight 1.0, the *StrokeCollection* exposes only one property, *Count*, which can be used to return the number of strokes that are currently held within the collection.

StrokeCollection Methods

The *StrokeCollection* exposes the following methods:

- **Add**   This allows you to add a new stroke to the collection.
- **Clear**   This clears the collection of strokes, which causes an immediate rerendering (thus clearing the Ink that was previously created).
- **GetBounds**   This returns a rectangle (in a *Rect* structure) that represents the bounding box of the strokes.
- **GetItem(index)**   This will retrieve the stroke that is stored at the specified index.
- **HitTest**   If you pass this method a *StylusPointCollection*, it will return the subset of strokes in the *StrokeCollection* that intersect with these points.
- **Insert**   This is similar to *Add*, except that it allows you to insert a new stroke to the collection at a specific collection index.
- **Remove**   This will remove a specific element from the *StrokeCollection*.
- **RemoveAt**   This will remove the indexed element from the *StrokeCollection*.

The *Stroke* Type

The *StrokeCollection* that you saw in the previous section is a collection of *Stroke* objects. A *Stroke* object represents a collection of points that corresponds to a stroke; the points are recorded with a single stylus action: stylus-down, stylus-move, stylus-up. These objects in turn have their own set of properties and methods.

Stroke Properties

The *Stroke* object exposes these properties:

- **DrawingAttributes**   Each stroke can have independent height, width, color, and outline color. These are set using the *DrawingAttributes* type. To use this type, you create an instance of a *DrawingAttributes* object, set these properties, and then add the new *DrawingAttributes* object to the stroke.

■ **StylusPoints**   This is a *StylusPointCollection* that contains the collection of *StylusPoint* objects that make up the stroke. The *StylusPoint* is discussed in the following section.

Stroke Methods

The *Stroke* object exposes the following Ink-specific methods:

■ **GetBounds**   This returns the bounding box of the *Stroke* as a *Rect* structure.

■ **HitTest**   If you pass this method a *StylusPointCollection*, and if any of those points intersect the *Stroke*, this method will return *true*; otherwise it will be *false*.

The *StylusPointCollection* Type

This collection hosts a set of *StylusPoint* objects. It is used to store the stylus points for a *Stroke*, or in some cases, it can be passed to methods such as the *HitTest* method to determine whether or not strokes intersect.

StylusPointCollection Properties

The *StylusPointCollection* exposes only one property—the *Count* property that returns a count of the stylus points that are held in this collection.

StylusPointCollection Methods

The *StylusPointCollection* object exposes these methods:

■ **add**   This method allows you to add a new *StylusPoint* to the end of the collection.

■ **addStylusPoints**   This method allows you to add an existing *StylusPointCollection* to the bottom of this collection.

■ **clear**   This removes all *StylusPoint* objects from the collection.

■ **getItem**   This gets a specific *StylusPoint* from the collection. Use it with an integer value representing the index of the item you want to reference such as *getItem(i)*.

■ **insert**   This inserts a new *StylusPoint* into the collection at the specified index.

■ **remove**   This removes a specific *StylusPoint* from the collection.

■ **removeAt**   This removes the *StylusPoint* at the specified index from the collection.

The *StylusPoint* Type

The *StylusPoint* type represents a single point that is collected while the user is Inking with their device—a pen, a mouse, or a touch screen. The point exposes a number of properties and methods for programmability.

StylusPoint Properties

The *StylusPoint* exposes the following properties:.

- The *Name* property allows you to name the point. This is a unique identifier. When points are generated by user input, they are unnamed.

- The *PressureFactor* property indicates the pressure that the user puts on the pen or touch screen to generate a stroke. When using a mouse, the pressure does not change from the default. The value is a double between 0.0 and 1.0, with a default value of 0.5. Based on the pressure factor, you can programmatically change the height and width of the *Stroke* through its *DrawingAttributes* property to give feedback to the user.

The coordinates of the stroke are returned using the *X* and *Y* properties. These are measured in pixels.

Mouse Event Arguments and Ink

When using Ink, events raised by the input device are treated as mouse events, and arguments received by your event handlers will be *MouseEventArgs*.

The *MouseEventArgs* object contains methods that allow you to query the stylus information—to see if it is a mouse, stylus, or some other input device—and that allow you to query for the collection of *StylusPoint* objects associated with this event.

Note that this is the same *MouseEventArgs* object that is associated with the *MouseEnter*, *MouseLeave*, *MouseLeftButtonDown*, *MouseLeftButtonUp*, and *MouseMove* events.

MouseEventArgs Properties

The *MouseEventArgs* object exposes two Boolean properties called *ctrl* and *shift*. These are *true* when the user holds down the equivalent key while raising the event.

MouseEventArgs Methods

The *MouseEventArgs* object exposes three methods:

- The *GetPosition* method takes an element as its parameter and returns a *Point* that represents the x- and y-coordinates of the mouse pointer relative to that element. If nothing is passed in, then the *Point* contains the coordinates relative to the position of the control that raised the event.

- The *GetStylusInfo* method returns a *StylusInfo* object that contains information about the state of the stylus. *StylusInfo* has the following properties:

  ❑ *IsInverted*: When a pen is inverted, it indicates that the user wants to use it to *erase* points instead of drawing them. This property returns *true* in that circumstance.

  ❑ *DeviceType*: This returns a string containing the device type–"Mouse", "Stylus", or "Touch".

- The *GetStylusPoints* method returns a clone of the stylus points that were collected since the last mouse event. This will be a *StylusPointCollection* type.

Using Ink in Silverlight

As we have mentioned, the term *Ink* refers to handwriting or drawing content that is provided by the user using the Ink-based devices we've mentioned, such as a digital pen, touch screen, or mouse. When they are used in a Silverlight application, these devices fill a *StrokeCollection* object with individual *Stroke* objects. In turn, a *Stroke* maintains a record the device's actions, such as a pen, that include, for example, the pen-down, pen-move, and pen-up actions. A *Stroke* will can represent a dot, a straight line, or a curve. It does this by maintaining a *StylusPointCollection* object, which contains *StylusPoint* objects that are collected from the digitizer associated with the pen, touch screen, or mouse. Attributes of the Ink are contained in the *DrawingAttributes* class.

As mentioned, Ink is collected by Silverlight using the *InkPresenter* class. This is effectively a subclass of the *Canvas* element, which also contains a collection of strokes in a *StrokeCollection*. When strokes are added to the *StrokeCollection*, then the *InkPresenter* will automatically render them using the pertinent *DrawingAttributes*.

You'll typically add the *InkPresenter* to your XAML for your application at design time, but the *Stroke* objects within the *StrokeCollection* will be added at run time using JavaScript.

Following is an example of using *InkPresenter* on a page, overlaying an image:

```
<Canvas xmlns="http://schemas.microsoft.com/client/2007"
        xmlns:x="http://schemas.microsoft.com/winfx/2006/xaml">
  <Image Source="sushi.jpg"></Image>
  <InkPresenter
    x:Name="inkEl"
    Background="transparent"
    Width="600" Height="400"
    MouseLeftButtonDown="inkMouseDown"
    MouseMove="inkMouseMove"
    MouseLeftButtonUp="inkMouseUp"/>
</Canvas>
```

The *InkPresenter* defines event handlers for *MouseLeftButtonDown*, *MouseMove*, and *MouseUp*. These will need JavaScript event handler functions that handle the "start inking," "draw ink," and "stop inking" actions.

> **Note**   Although inking can be done with a pen, a touch screen, or a mouse, the API documentation uses the term "Mouse" throughout.

Before we look at these JavaScript event handler functions, there is a little housekeeping we need to provide that will declare the global variables necessary to support these actions:

```
var theInk;      // Reference to the ink presenter
var newStroke;   // Reference to a stroke
var theControl;  // Reference to the Silverlight control
function handleLoad(control, userContext, rootElement)
{
    // The Load event returns a reference to the control
    // But other event handlers do not. So we're going
    // to make a reference to the control here
    theControl = control;

    // Here we will create a reference to the ink element
    theInk = control.content.findName("inkEl");
}
```

The Ink actions I mentioned will be supported by functions that will use these helper variables for the Ink presenter, the current stroke, and the Silverlight control itself. When the Silverlight control loads, it triggers the *handleLoad* function. This takes a reference to the Silverlight control as one of its parameters, but since the event handlers that we are implementing for managing the mouse do not, we'll need to save a reference to the Silverlight control from within the *handleLoad* function. While processing in *handleLoad*, you might as well also get a reference to the ink presenter by finding it based on its name (*inkEl*). This saves you from having to issue a *getHost* to get a reference to the parent UI element control to find the ink presenter in each event handler invocation.

Now we're ready to learn more about the event handlers. First, let's look at what happens when the *mouseLeftButtonDown* event fires, in effect causing *inkMouseDown* to run. You'll want to capture the mouse movement in a fashion similar to the drag-and-drop processing you learned about in Chapter 5, "Programming Silverlight with JavaScript." After you have captured the mouse input, you will create a new *Stroke* that contains a *DrawingAttributes* object that defines the visual characteristics of this stroke. In the example presented here, *DrawingAttributes* for the stroke will provide it with a *Width* of 2, a *Height* of 2, a fill color of *White*, and an outline color of *White*. The *MouseEventArgs* type in Silverlight supports a *getStylusPoints* method, as you saw earlier in this chapter, that takes the *InkPresenter* as its sole parameter. This method returns a *StylusPointCollection* type that can be used with the Stroke's *AddStylusPoints* method. You then add the stroke to the ink presenter's strokes collection. You can see the code here:

```
function inkMouseDown(sender,args)
    {
        // Capture the mouse.
        theInk.CaptureMouse();

        // Create a new stroke.
        newStroke = theControl.content.createFromXaml('<Stroke/>');

        // Assign a new drawing attributes element to the stroke.
        // This, as its name suggests, defines how the stroke will appear
        var da = theControl.content.CreateFromXaml('<DrawingAttributes/>');
        newStroke.DrawingAttributes = da;

        // Now that the stroke has drawing attributes,
        // let's define them...
        newStroke.DrawingAttributes.Width = 2;
        newStroke.DrawingAttributes.Height = 2;
        newStroke.DrawingAttributes.Color = "White";
        newStroke.DrawingAttributes.OutlineColor = "White";


        newStroke.StylusPoints.AddStylusPoints(args.GetStylusPoints(theInk));
        theInk.Strokes.Add(newStroke);
    }
}
```

Now as you move the mouse over the canvas, if you are currently drawing a stroke (i.e., *newStroke* is not *null*), then you want to generate new points to add to this stroke, representing the track over which the mouse moved. Following is the code for this:

```
// Add the new points to the Stroke we're working with.
function inkMouseMove(sender,args)
{
    if (newStroke != null)
    {
        newStroke.StylusPoints.AddStylusPoints(args.GetStylusPoints(theInk));
    }
}
```

Finally, the *mouseLeftButtonUp* event will fire after you finish the stroke by releasing the mouse button (or by lifting the pen from the screen). Then you want to clear the stroke and release the mouse capture. When the *newStroke* variable has been set to *null*, the mouse (or pen) movement across the screen will no longer collect points to add to the stroke, and stroke output will therefore not be drawn. Here's the code:

```
function inkMouseUp(sender,args)
{
    // Set the stroke to null
    newStroke = null;

    // Release the mouse
    theInk.releaseMouseCapture();
}
```

Figure 6-3 shows an example of an application before Ink annotation was added to it; Figure 6-4 shows the same application after Ink annotation has been added to it—the annotation was drawn on it using a mouse or pen.

Figure 6-3 Running the Silverlight Inked application.

Figure 6-4   The Silverlight Inked application with Ink applied.

Summary

In this chapter, you looked at the Ink support that is available in Silverlight 1.0. You learned about the devices that are supported to add Ink annotation and how they all map to the *Mouse* type in the API as well as in the API documentation. You explored the PageTurn sample from the Silverlight Web site and saw how it uses Inking for image annotation. Next, you browsed through the set of classes that support Inking in Silverlight, including the *StylusPoint* object and its collection, the Stroke object and its collection, and the *InkPresenter* object itself. Finally, you created a simple Ink application.

In Chapter 7, we will focus on server programming and explore how to generate Silverlight applications on a server using ASP.NET, Java Enterprise Edition (J2EE or JEE), and Personal Hypertext Processor (PHP).

Chapter 7
Silverlight Server Programming

One of the characteristics of Silverlight that makes it such a powerful tool is that the XAML that provides the structural framework is XML and thus can be generated by a server. In the examples you've seen so far, the XAML is static, and a document is generated by a designer using a tool such as Expression Blend. However, you aren't limited to using static XAML, and you can enable a whole range of new scenarios by dynamically generating your XAML and having it sent to your users in response to application logic or state.

For example, if you want to build an application that provides weather details in XAML, you couldn't effectively do this with static XAML without having to create a complicated system to generate different XAML documents periodically for each of your users' locations so users could download the appropriate document upon request. It is far easier to generate an application template and then fill in the placeholders within the application user interface (UI) using information gleaned from a server.

There are many different languages that can be used to build server applications, but this chapter will concentrate only on the three major ones: Personal Home Page (PHP), Java, and ASP.NET. We'll examine how to generate XAML in each of these languages, first in a generic sense and then using the specific weather information example.

Silverlight and PHP

PHP (available for download from *http://www.php.net*) is a simple yet powerful scripting language that can be used easily to template XAML. It typically takes PHP code as its input and creates Web pages as its output. You can use the same method to generate XAML dynamically. If you aren't familiar with PHP, the following sections will provide you with a basic introduction.

Your First PHP Page

PHP can be used to generate Web pages dynamically based on input parameters. So, for example, consider this simple HTML page:

```
<HTML>
<HEAD>
</HEAD>
<BODY>
<H1>Hello, World!</H1>
</BODY>
</HTML>
```

This renders a simple HTML page containing the text "Hello, World!", which you can see in Figure 7-1.

Figure 7-1   Simple "Hello World" Web page.

You can make this simple page dynamic using PHP. In this case, the page takes a parameter and the PHP preprocessor fills it in. Following is the PHP code:

```
<HTML>
<HEAD>
</HEAD>
<BODY>
<H1>Hello, <?php echo($_REQUEST['name']);?>!</H1>
<BODY>
</HTML>
```

Here you can see the HTML markup code has some embedded PHP code that retrieves the URL parameter *name* and then writes it to the response stream using the *echo* command. So, if you browse to this page, passing it a value for *name*, then the PHP processor will dynamically render the page markup. The following URL parameter, for example, can be seen in the display shown in Figure 7-2:

http://localhost/phptext/Hello.php?name=Laurence

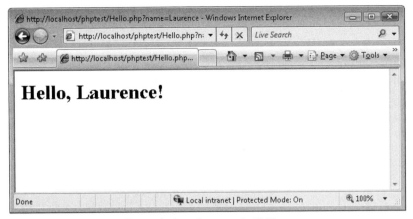

Figure 7-2   Dynamically rendering the page in PHP.

PHP and XAML Case Study

The same principle can apply to XAML. You can easily create an XAML template for how you would like your content to be presented using Expression Blend. This template can then be used within a PHP page. If you need repeating functionality to present the content, as with a list, you can create that content with a PHP loop.

This is best demonstrated by example. PHP—along with Apache, MySQL, and Linux—is a core element of the famous LAMP stack, so let's take a look at how we would build a PHP/MySQL application that could run on any Web server or operating system that supports LAMP. (The acronym comes from the first letters of Linux, Apache, MySQL, and PHP.) We'll actually be building a "Windows IIS MySQL PHP" application, with the unfortunate acronym WIMP!

Building the Server-Side Database

In this case, MySQL is used to build a server-side database of names and addresses. MySQL can be downloaded and installed from *http://www.mysql.com*, and there is a freely available "community" edition that is ideal for developers to use for experimentation.

In addition to this, there is a suite of GUI tools, such as the MySQL Administrator and MySQL Query Browser, available for building and populating sample databases. Instruction in using these tools is beyond the scope of this book, but you can check out the extensive documentation on the MySQL.com Web site if you're not familiar with them.

Figure 7-3 shows the MySQL Table Editor and how it is used to define a simple table containing names and addresses.

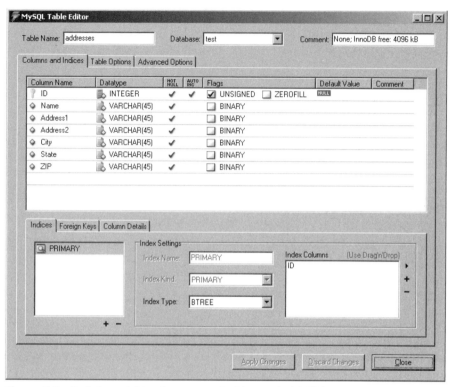

Figure 7-3 Defining a table of names and addresses in MySQL.

You can use the MySQL Query Browser to edit the contents of the table. Simply click the Edit button at the bottom of the application's user interface (see Figure 7-4), and then you can type in sample name and address data, as shown in Figure 7-4.

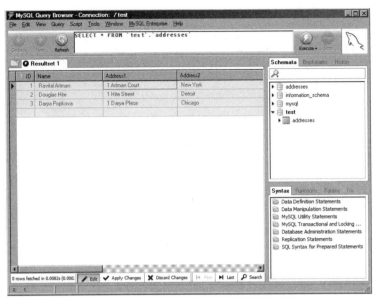

Figure 7-4   Adding table data with the MySQL Query Browser.

With some data in your database for PHP to expose, it's time to couple the data with your XAML template. In the next section, you'll learn how to build the template using Expression Blend.

Building a XAML Template

Now that we have our data, let's think about how we're going to present it using XAML. Expression Blend is a great visual editor for XAML—and Figure 7-5 shows an example of a XAML template that we can use to provide our users with the name and address data from our table.

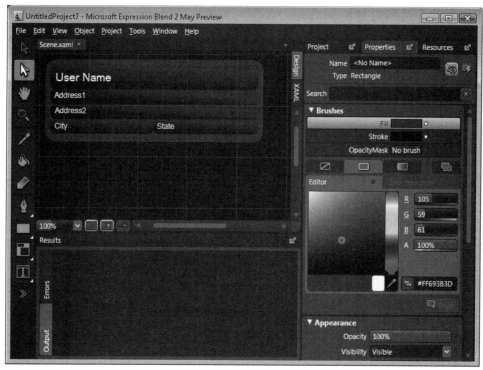

Figure 7-5 Designing a XAML template with Expression Blend.

The resulting XAML represents a collection of *Canvas*, *Rectangle*, and *TextBlock* objects. The full XAML for the template shown in Figure 7-5 is provided in Listing 7-1. Note that the XAML contains an enclosing canvas as the root node, and then another canvas that contains the rest of the UI elements. It is this canvas that will be repeated for multiple records.

Listing 7-1 XAML Address Application Template

```
<Canvas
  xmlns="http://schemas.microsoft.com/client/2007"
  xmlns:x="http://schemas.microsoft.com/winfx/2006/xaml"
  Width="640" Height="480"
  Background="#FF460608">
  <Canvas Width="352" Height="128" Canvas.Left="10" Canvas.Top="8" >
    <Rectangle Fill="#FF693B3D" Stroke="#FF000000" StrokeThickness="0"
      RadiusX="16" RadiusY="16" Width="352" Height="128" Canvas.Top="1"/>
    <Rectangle Stroke="#FF000000" StrokeThickness="0" RadiusX="8"
      RadiusY="8" Width="336" Height="40" Canvas.Left="8" Canvas.Top="8">
      <Rectangle.Fill>
        <LinearGradientBrush EndPoint="0.518,0.175" StartPoint="0.515,0.825">
          <GradientStop Color="#FF460608" Offset="0"/>
          <GradientStop Color="#FF841316" Offset="1"/>
        </LinearGradientBrush>
      </Rectangle.Fill>
    </Rectangle>
```

```xml
<TextBlock x:Name="txtName" Width="312" Height="24"
  Canvas.Left="16" Canvas.Top="16" FontFamily="Arial Unicode MS"
  FontSize="18" FontWeight="Normal" Foreground="#FFFFFFFF"
  Text="User Name" TextWrapping="Wrap"/>
<Rectangle Stroke="#FF000000" StrokeThickness="0"
  RadiusX="8" RadiusY="8" Width="336" Height="23"
  Canvas.Left="8" Canvas.Top="48">
  <Rectangle.Fill>
    <LinearGradientBrush EndPoint="0.518,0.175" StartPoint="0.515,0.825">
      <GradientStop Color="#FF460608" Offset="0"/>
      <GradientStop Color="#FF841316" Offset="1"/>
    </LinearGradientBrush>
  </Rectangle.Fill>
</Rectangle>
<TextBlock x:Name="txtAddr1" Width="312" Height="24"
  FontFamily="Arial Unicode MS" FontSize="12" FontWeight="Normal"
  Foreground="#FFFFFFFF" Text="Address1"
  TextWrapping="Wrap" Canvas.Left="14" Canvas.Top="48"/>
<Rectangle Stroke="#FF000000" StrokeThickness="0"
  RadiusX="8" RadiusY="8" Width="336"
  Height="23" Canvas.Left="8" Canvas.Top="71">
  <Rectangle.Fill>
    <LinearGradientBrush EndPoint="0.518,0.175" StartPoint="0.515,0.825">
      <GradientStop Color="#FF460608" Offset="0"/>
      <GradientStop Color="#FF841316" Offset="1"/>
    </LinearGradientBrush>
  </Rectangle.Fill>
</Rectangle>
<TextBlock x:Name="txtAddr2" Width="312" Height="24"
  FontFamily="Arial Unicode MS" FontSize="12"
  FontWeight="Normal" Foreground="#FFFFFFFF"
  Text="Address2" TextWrapping="Wrap"
  Canvas.Left="15" Canvas.Top="72"/>
<Rectangle Stroke="#FF000000" StrokeThickness="0"
  RadiusX="8" RadiusY="8" Width="168" Height="23"
  Canvas.Left="176" Canvas.Top="94">
  <Rectangle.Fill>
    <LinearGradientBrush EndPoint="0.518,0.175" StartPoint="0.515,0.825">
      <GradientStop Color="#FF460608" Offset="0"/>
      <GradientStop Color="#FF841316" Offset="1"/>
    </LinearGradientBrush>
  </Rectangle.Fill>
</Rectangle>
<Rectangle Stroke="#FF000000" StrokeThickness="0"
  RadiusX="8" RadiusY="8" Width="168"
  Height="23" Canvas.Left="8" Canvas.Top="94">
  <Rectangle.Fill>
    <LinearGradientBrush EndPoint="0.518,0.175" StartPoint="0.515,0.825">
      <GradientStop Color="#FF460608" Offset="0"/>
      <GradientStop Color="#FF841316" Offset="1"/>
    </LinearGradientBrush>
  </Rectangle.Fill>
</Rectangle>
<TextBlock x:Name="txtCity" Width="144" Height="24"
  FontFamily="Arial Unicode MS" FontSize="12"
```

```
              FontWeight="Normal" Foreground="#FFFFFFFF" Text="City"
              TextWrapping="Wrap" Canvas.Left="15" Canvas.Top="96"/>
          <TextBlock x:Name="txtState" Width="144" Height="24"
              FontFamily="Arial Unicode MS" FontSize="12"
              FontWeight="Normal" Foreground="#FFFFFFFF" Text="State"
              TextWrapping="Wrap" Canvas.Left="182" Canvas.Top="96"/>
      </Canvas>
    </Canvas>
```

This second canvas (hereafter called the *container*) has its *Canvas.Top* property set to 8 pixels, and its *Height* set to 128 pixels. Therefore, if we want to stack other instances of this canvas below the first, we need to locate the *Canvas.Top* for the second container at 136 (128 + 8), and then we need to locate the next container at 264 (128 + 128 + 8), and so forth.

The container canvas contains all the UI elements, but the UI elements need to have distinct names in XAML. You can see that each *TextBlock* has been named, using the *x:Name* attribute in this XAML example. When we clone the container, we'll need to edit this XAML so that it has distinct names for these nodes. The naming algorithm will be simple—we will use an index appended to the end of the name. So, for example, the *x:Name* value *txtState* recorded in the template will become *txtState1* for the first database row, and then it will be *txtState2* for the next database row, and so forth.

Cloning these elements in PHP is very straightforward, as you'll see in the next section.

Generating XAML from PHP and MySQL

MySQL implements page parsing, which means that when the server is instructed to return the page, MySQL will write formatted data to the response buffer. When MySQL encounters a special opening tag (*<?php*), it passes the processing over to the PHP parser, which then executes the code the PHP processor finds there until it encounters a closing tag (*?>*). This makes the combination of MySQL and PHP ideally suited for rendering templated content. You simply put the template for the content that you want to generate into a file with the .php extension, and any place in the file you need to fill in some data-bound placeholders, you place the necessary PHP logic within the PHP opening and closing tags (*<?php* and *?>* respectively).

PHP logic can contain loops, and if you have a loop statement followed by some content, then you'll find the content will be written out many times. The loop can traverse open-close couplets—so, for example, you can do the following:

```
<?php
for($i=0; $i<100; $i++)
{ // Loop opening brace
// Exiting PHP, though we haven't closed our loop yet!
?>
<H1>My Text Line is <?php echo $i; ?></H1>
<?php
```

```
} // Now we close our loop
?>
```

This will repeat the HTML content (the text within and including the *<H1>* tag) 100 times. You can see that the *<?php ... ?>* couplets do not need to completely surround the text, which is useful when you couple PHP and XAML.

With XAML, our enclosing canvas can be contained within a loop, like this:

```
<?php
for($i=0; $i<100; $i++)
{ // Loop opening brace
// Exiting PHP, though we haven't closed our loop yet!
?>
<Canvas>
...
</Canvas>
<?php
} // Now we close our loop
?>
```

With this code, the XAML will be written 100 times! This makes PHP a powerful templating language for Silverlight.

To return to our example, let's take a look at what it takes to connect to the database, run a query against it, and write out the appropriate number of XAML *Canvas* elements based on the number of returned results. We'll also edit the contents of the *TextBlock* elements within the canvas to display the information from the database as well as adjust the *TextBlock* name so that they are unique.

Ultimately, you will build a PHP page that generates XAML for you. This will then be used as the source for the Silverlight control, which will render the XAML. However, to make it a little more interesting, we'll modify the generator to accept a parameter (a state value for our example) so that it returns information only for the people with an address in that state. This will make it a truly dynamic XAML generator.

First, we'll need to have Silverlight recognize the output from PHP as XML. To do that, you have to set the MIME type of the output content. This is done in PHP with the header command like this:

```
header('Content-type: text/xml');
```

To retrieve a request string parameter (i.e., *http://server/script.php?param=value*) using PHP, you use the $_REQUEST array. So, if we want to read the value of the parameter *State*, we'll use code like the following:

```
$State=$_REQUEST['State'];
```

Versions 4.x of PHP have the MySQL command set built in. Versions 5.x and greater require you to specify the MySQL command set as an extension. Regardless of which you use, the PHP syntax is the same.

To connect to the *localhost* server with the username *user* and the password *password*, you use the *mysql_connect* command:

```
$con = mysql_connect("localhost", "user", "password");
```

The server can contain more than one database, so you select the database you want to work with using the *mysql_select_db* command:

```
mysql_select_db("test", $con); // "test" is the database name
```

Then, to run a query against this database, you use the *mysql_query* command and pass it a string containing the actual SQL query. The result set will be returned back as an array of arrays of values. Following is an example:

```
$result = mysql_query($sqlString);
```

The *mysql_fetch_array* then splits this into rows, and you can use a *while* loop to cycle through each row, as shown in the following example:

```
while($row = mysql_fetch_array($result))
{
...
}
```

Therefore, given this scenario, here is the algorithm we want to follow:

1. Set the MIME type to *text/xml*.

2. Get the input parameter (the state).

3. Write out the "root" *Canvas* starting tag.

4. Use the input parameter to build a query.

5. Run the query and get the result set.

6. For each row in the result set:

    a. Fill *Text* attributes of *TextBlocks* with relevant data from database field.

    b. Write out the XAML of the container XAML.

    c. Fill *x:Name* attributes with unique ID based on row count.

7. Close the "root" *Canvas* tag.

The full PHP page to accomplish this is shown in Listing 7-2. The PHP markup within the XAML block is shown in bold type.

Listing 7-2   PHP Code to Generate XAML

```php
<?php
header('Content-type: text/xml');
$State=$_REQUEST['State'];
?>
<Canvas
  xmlns="http://schemas.microsoft.com/client/2007"
  xmlns:x="http://schemas.microsoft.com/winfx/2006/xaml"
  Width="640" Height="480"
  Background="#FF460608"

  >
<?php
$height=128;
$top=8;
$i=0;
$con = mysql_connect("localhost", "user", "password");
mysql_select_db("test",$con);
$sqlString = "SELECT * from addresses";
if($State!="")
{
    $sqlString = $sqlString . " WHERE State = '" . $State . "'";
}
$result = mysql_query($sqlString);
while($row = mysql_fetch_array($result))
{
?>
    <Canvas Width="352" Height="128" Canvas.Left="10"
        Canvas.Top="<?php echo($top + ($height*$i)); ?>" >        <Rectangle
Fill="#FF693B3D" Stroke="#FF000000"
        StrokeThickness="0" RadiusX="16" RadiusY="16"
        Width="352" Height="128" Canvas.Top="1"/>
      <Rectangle Stroke="#FF000000" StrokeThickness="0"
        RadiusX="8" RadiusY="8" Width="336" Height="40"
        Canvas.Left="8" Canvas.Top="8">
        <Rectangle.Fill>
          <LinearGradientBrush EndPoint="0.518,0.175" StartPoint="0.515,0.825">
            <GradientStop Color="#FF460608" Offset="0"/>
            <GradientStop Color="#FF841316" Offset="1"/>
          </LinearGradientBrush>
        </Rectangle.Fill>
      </Rectangle>
      <TextBlock x:Name="txtName<?php echo $i; ?>" Width="312" Height="24"
        Canvas.Left="16" Canvas.Top="16"
        FontFamily="Arial Unicode MS" FontSize="18"
        FontWeight="Normal" Foreground="#FFFFFFFF"
        Text="<?php echo($row['Name']); ?>"
        TextWrapping="Wrap"/>
      <Rectangle Stroke="#FF000000" StrokeThickness="0"
        RadiusX="8" RadiusY="8" Width="336"
        Height="23" Canvas.Left="8" Canvas.Top="48">
      <Rectangle.Fill>
        <LinearGradientBrush EndPoint="0.518,0.175" StartPoint="0.515,0.825">
          <GradientStop Color="#FF460608" Offset="0"/>
          <GradientStop Color="#FF841316" Offset="1"/>
```

```
        </LinearGradientBrush>
      </Rectangle.Fill>
    </Rectangle>
  <TextBlock x:Name="txtAddr1<?php echo $i; ?>" Width="312"
    Height="24" FontFamily="Arial Unicode MS" FontSize="12"
    FontWeight="Normal" Foreground="#FFFFFFFF"
    Text="<?php echo($row['Address1']); ?>" TextWrapping="Wrap"
    Canvas.Left="14" Canvas.Top="48"/>
  <Rectangle Stroke="#FF000000" StrokeThickness="0"
    RadiusX="8" RadiusY="8" Width="336" Height="23"
    Canvas.Left="8" Canvas.Top="71">
    <Rectangle.Fill>
      <LinearGradientBrush EndPoint="0.518,0.175" StartPoint="0.515,0.825">
        <GradientStop Color="#FF460608" Offset="0"/>
        <GradientStop Color="#FF841316" Offset="1"/>
      </LinearGradientBrush>
    </Rectangle.Fill>
  </Rectangle>
  <TextBlock x:Name="txtAddr2<?php echo $i; ?>" Width="312"
    Height="24" FontFamily="Arial Unicode MS"
    FontSize="12" FontWeight="Normal"
    Foreground="#FFFFFFFF"
    Text="<?php echo($row['Address2']); ?>" TextWrapping="Wrap"
    Canvas.Left="15" Canvas.Top="72"/>
  <Rectangle Stroke="#FF000000" StrokeThickness="0"
    RadiusX="8" RadiusY="8" Width="168" Height="23"
    Canvas.Left="176" Canvas.Top="94">
    <Rectangle.Fill>
      <LinearGradientBrush EndPoint="0.518,0.175" StartPoint="0.515,0.825">
        <GradientStop Color="#FF460608" Offset="0"/>
        <GradientStop Color="#FF841316" Offset="1"/>
      </LinearGradientBrush>
    </Rectangle.Fill>
  </Rectangle>
  <Rectangle Stroke="#FF000000" StrokeThickness="0"
    RadiusX="8" RadiusY="8" Width="168"
    Height="23" Canvas.Left="8" Canvas.Top="94">
    <Rectangle.Fill>
      <LinearGradientBrush EndPoint="0.518,0.175" StartPoint="0.515,0.825">
        <GradientStop Color="#FF460608" Offset="0"/>
        <GradientStop Color="#FF841316" Offset="1"/>
      </LinearGradientBrush>
    </Rectangle.Fill>
  </Rectangle>
  <TextBlock x:Name="txtCity<?php echo $i; ?>" Width="144"
    Height="24" FontFamily="Arial Unicode MS"
    FontSize="12" FontWeight="Normal" Foreground="#FFFFFFFF"
    Text="<?php echo($row['City']); ?>" TextWrapping="Wrap"
    Canvas.Left="15" Canvas.Top="96"/>
  <TextBlock x:Name="txtState<?php echo $i; ?>" Width="144"
    Height="24" FontFamily="Arial Unicode MS" FontSize="12"
    FontWeight="Normal" Foreground="#FFFFFFFF"
    Text="<?php echo($row['State']); ?>"
    TextWrapping="Wrap" Canvas.Left="182" Canvas.Top="96"/>
</Canvas>
```

```
<?php
$i++;
}
?>
</Canvas>
```

Building a PHP Page to Deliver Silverlight

As you saw in the previous section, when using PHP, the server outputs content directly until it sees the opening tag(<?*php*), at which point it references the PHP interpreter, which then runs the code contained within opening and the closing tag (?>).

The PHP code typically is used to activate HTML code, and since Silverlight is delivered from HTML, it is a straightforward process to edit an HTML page to add these tags and rename the page with a .php file extension. So, to deliver Silverlight using PHP, you want a page that includes Silverlight.js and createSilverlight.js in the usual way, calling *createSilverlight* to instantiate the Silverlight control.

Because we want this page to accept a parameter for a particular state so that the user can access the names and addresses in the database by state, this page must be designed to accept a parameter and then use the parameter to create Silverlight content using the XAML source PHP that you saw in the previous step, which, fortunately, is quite simple in PHP. To display the rendered XAML, all you need to do is set the *content* property of the Silverlight control to your application's Uniform Resource Indicator (URI), and Silverlight will contact the server at that URI, accept the resulting XAML, and render it.

Following is an example of a complete PHP page that generates HTML:

```
<html xmlns="http://www.w3.org/1999/xhtml">
<head>
<title>SilverlightJSApplication2</title>

<script type="text/javascript" src="Silverlight.js"></script>
<script type="text/javascript" src="createSilverlight.js"></script>
<script type="text/javascript">
  function handleLoad(control, userContext, rootElement)
  { <?php
  if(!isset($_REQUEST['State']))
    $State="";
  else
    $State=$_REQUEST['State'];
?>
  control.source = "http://localhost/phptest/xaml.php?State=<?php echo($State) ?>";
  }
</script>
</head>
<body>
    <div id="SilverlightControlHost">
      <script type="text/javascript">
```

```
            createSilverlight();
        </script>
    </div>
</body>
</html>
```

Figures 7-6 and 7-7 show this PHP page is rendered in the browser, using Silverlight, for addresses in New York (NY in the database) and Washington (WA).

Figure 7-6 PHP application-rendered content for addresses in New York.

Figure 7-7   PHP application-rendered content for addresses in Washington.

Silverlight and Java

The Java language is compiled into byte code that is either interpreted or Just-In-Time (JIT) compiled and executed at run time on a virtual machine. This makes it ideal for server environments, particularly where diverse operating systems are present in the data center. Java is supported on nearly every major operating system.

There are many ways to build server applications in Java and its associated Enterprise edition, commonly called *J2EE* or just *JEE*. One method is to use Java Server Pages (JSP), which are similar in concept to PHP, in which the desired output is marked up with code that will execute at run time. So, to produce browsable HTML, you use standard HTML markup, but activate it by placing JSP tags within it that will execute as the page is being rendered. Another is the Java *Servlet*, which is an application that runs on a server and accepts parameters via HTTP.

The openness of Silverlight makes it easy to build applications incorporating both Silverlight and Java. You can use JSP technology to build pages that contain Silverlight content, and server-based technologies such as servlets are ideal for generating the XAML that is rendered by the browser.

To demonstrate how to build Silverlight applications in a Java-based infrastructure, we will use both of these technologies. First we will investigate how to build a JSP page to deliver the Silverlight control, and then we will build a servlet to generate XAML that the Silverlight control renders.

Building a XAML Source Servlet

A *servlet* is an application that extends the *HttpServlet* class in the *javax.servlet* namespace. It exposes two functions, *doGet* and *doPost*, that are used to capture HTTP-GET and HTTP-POST commands respectively. Each of these functions takes an *HTTPRequest* and *HTTPResponse* object. The former is used to capture the details of the request; the latter controls the response. Typically, you'll read parameters from the *HTTPRequest* object and write output to the *HTTPResponse* object. Following is an example of these functions:

```
protected void doGet(HttpServletRequest request, HttpServletResponse response)
    throws ServletException, IOException {
        // Handle GET
    }

protected void doPost(HttpServletRequest request, HttpServletResponse response)
    throws ServletException, IOException {
        // Handle POST
    }
```

In a typical design pattern, you would write a helper function that accepts the request and response objects, and then the *doGet* and *doPost* methods call that function. In this manner, regardless of how the servlet is invoked, you'll run the same code.

For this example, the servlet will take a XAML document as a template and then use the XML application programming interfaces (APIs) in Java to manipulate the document, filling in its contents with the results of a database query.

Following is an example of the simple XAML document that is used in this case study:

```
<Canvas
  xmlns="http://schemas.microsoft.com/winfx/2006/xaml/presentation"
  xmlns:x="http://schemas.microsoft.com/winfx/2006/xaml"
  Width="200" Height="80"
  Background="#FF000000">
  <TextBlock x:Name="txtName" Width="200" Height="24"
      Canvas.Left="24" Canvas.Top="8" Foreground="#FFEFB9B9"
      Text="Name" TextWrapping="Wrap"/>
  <TextBlock x:Name="txtCity" Width="200" Height="24"
      Canvas.Left="24" Canvas.Top="40" Foreground="#FFEFB9B9"
      Text="City" TextWrapping="Wrap"/>
  <TextBlock x:Name="txtCountry" Width="200" Height="24"
      Canvas.Left="24" Canvas.Top="72" Foreground="#FFEFB9B9"
      Text="Country" TextWrapping="Wrap"/>
</Canvas>
```

This XAML contains three *TextBlock* elements. The servlet will query the customers database in the Northwind database and fill these *TextBlock* elements with the results. The query takes the customer ID as a parameter and uses it to pull the relevant customer record. The customer record data of interest include the customer's contact name, city, and country.

> **Note**   If you don't already have the Northwind database, you can download it from the
> Microsoft Developer Network (MSDN) at *http://www.microsoft.com/downloads/*
> *details.aspx?FamilyID=06616212-0356-46A0-8DA2-EEBC53A68034&displaylang=en.*

To fill the *TextBlock* elements, we'll need to locate them in the XAML document. When you use
the Java XML APIs to find nodes based on an XPath, you will need to define a namespace prefix for elements in the default namespace, so you will notice later that elements in the default
namespace (i.e., <TextBlock>) will be referred to using a run-time-added default namespace
prefix (i.e., <d:TextBlock>).

So, in Java, we will use the XML APIs to find the node that we want to edit based on their
name—for example, the TextBlock that contains the country is called "txtCountry," and once
we have it, we'll change its value. So, to generate our application's XAML, the helper function
will perform the following steps:

1. Get the input parameter. If it is *null*, set it to a default.

2. Set the output MIME type to *text/xml*.

3. Create an XML document and load the template XAML file.. In this example, the XAML
   is saved into a document called template.xml.

4. Open the SQL Server database and query the Northwind Customers table for a customer matching the input parameter.

5. There will be a maximum of one record to be read, so read it.

6. Use the XPath of the ContactName node to find it and then replace its contents with the
   value of the ContactName field read from the database.

7. Use the XPath of the City node to find it and then replace its contents with the value of
   the City field read from the database.

8. Use the XPath of the Country node to find it and then replace its contents with the value
   of the Country field read from the DB.

9. Write out the XML to the response stream.

Keep this algorithm in mind as you look at Listing 7-3, which shows the helper function code
the servlet uses to generate XAML.

Listing 7-3   Java Code to Generate XAML

```
protected void processRequest(HttpServletRequest request,
        HttpServletResponse response)
    throws ServletException, IOException {
    try
        {
        String strID = request.getParameter("ID");
        if(strID==null)
```

```
            strID="ALFKI";
        DocumentBuilderFactory factory = DocumentBuilderFactory.newInstance();
        factory.setNamespaceAware(true);
        response.setContentType("text/xml");
        PrintWriter out = response.getWriter();
        DocumentBuilder builder = factory.newDocumentBuilder();
        String uri = getServletContext().getRealPath("template.xml");
        Document doc = builder.parse(uri);
        DOMSource domSource = new DOMSource(doc);
        StreamResult streamResult = new StreamResult(out);
        TransformerFactory tf = TransformerFactory.newInstance();
        Transformer serializer = tf.newTransformer();
        XPathFactory xpFactory = XPathFactory.newInstance();
        XPath xpath = xpFactory.newXPath();
        xpath.setNamespaceContext(new DefaultNameSpaceContext());
        String strContactName="";
        String strCity="";
        String strCountry="";
        java.lang.Class.forName("com.microsoft.sqlserver.jdbc.SQLServerDriver");
        Connection c =
java.sql.DriverManager.getConnection("jdbc:sqlserver://
localhost\\SQLEXPRESS;databasename=Northwind;user=javauser;password=javauser;");
        String SQL =
"Select ContactName, City, Country from Customers where CustomerID = ?";
        PreparedStatement pstmt = c.prepareStatement(SQL);
        pstmt.setString(1, strID);
        ResultSet rs = pstmt.executeQuery();
        while (rs.next()) {
            strContactName = rs.getString("ContactName");
            strCity=rs.getString("City");
            strCountry=rs.getString("Country");
            String strXPath = "//d:TextBlock[@x:Name='txtName']";
            XPathExpression expr = xpath.compile(strXPath);
            Object result = expr.evaluate(doc,XPathConstants.NODESET);
            NodeList nodes = (NodeList) result;
            Node ndeT1 =
              nodes.item(0).getAttributes().getNamedItem("Text");
            ndeT1.setNodeValue(strContactName);
            strXPath = "//d:TextBlock[@x:Name='txtCity']";
            expr = xpath.compile(strXPath);
            result = expr.evaluate(doc,XPathConstants.NODESET);
            nodes = (NodeList) result;
            ndeT1 =
              nodes.item(0).getAttributes().getNamedItem("Text");
            ndeT1.setNodeValue(strCity);
            strXPath = "//d:TextBlock[@x:Name='txtCountry']";
            expr = xpath.compile(strXPath);
            result = expr.evaluate(doc,XPathConstants.NODESET);
            nodes = (NodeList) result;
            ndeT1 =
              nodes.item(0).getAttributes().getNamedItem("Text");
            ndeT1.setNodeValue(strCountry);
            }
            rs.close();
            pstmt.close();
```

```
            serializer.transform(domSource, streamResult);
                out.close();
        }
        catch(Exception ex)
        {
            ex.printStackTrace();
        }

    }
```

You can see the results of running this servlet (in the Tomcat application server) in Figure 7-8.

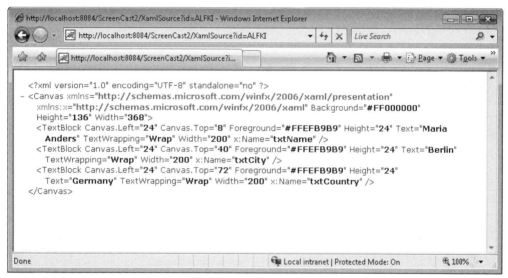

Figure 7-8 Generating XAML from a servlet.

Delivering Silverlight from JSP

To build a JSP page, you build an HTML page and then edit it with JSP markup for the parts where you want to execute page logic. In this case, you want to deliver a Silverlight solution, and you typically would do this by importing the *Silverlight.js* and *createSilverlight.js* script libraries and then calling *createSilverlight* within a named DIV.

However, this JSP page is going to do a little more—it is going to accept a parameter, and then it is going to use this parameter to build the XAML source element that you created earlier. To do this, you write Java code and embed it using the JSP <% and %> tags. You can see the full JSP page code in Listing 7-4.

Listing 7-4 JSP Code to Deliver Silverlight Content

```jsp
<%@page contentType="text/html"%>
<%@page pageEncoding="UTF-8"%>
<!DOCTYPE HTML PUBLIC "-//W3C//DTD HTML 4.01 Transitional//EN"
    "http://www.w3.org/TR/html4/loose.dtd">

<html>
    <head>
        <meta http-equiv="Content-Type" content="text/html; charset=UTF-8">
        <script type="text/javascript" src="js/silverlight.js"></script>
        <script type="text/javascript" src="js/createSilverlight.js"></script>
        <script type="text/javascript">
            function handleLoad(control, userContext, rootElement)
            {
                <%
                    String strValue="";
                    if (request.getParameter("ID") == null) {
                        strValue = "ALFKI";
                    } else {
                        strValue = request.getParameter("ID");
                    }
                %>
                control.source =
                  "http://localhost:8084/XamlSource?ID=
                  <% out.print(strValue); %>";
            }
        </script>
        <title>JSP Page</title>
    </head>
    <body>

    <h1>Silverlight JSP Page</h1>

    <div id="slContent">
        <script type="text/javascript">
            createSilverlight();
        </script>
    </div>
    </body>
</html>
```

You can see how this page looks in Figures 7-9 and 7-10. Note the parameter "AROUT" is passed to the JSP page in the first page's query string, whereas "ALFKI" is passed to the second page.

Figure 7-9   Running the JSP with the ID parameter AROUT.

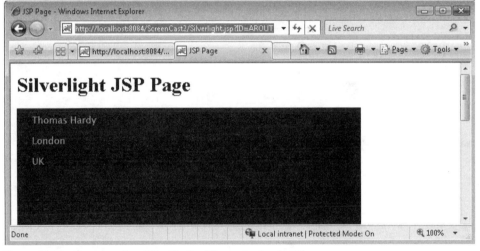

Figure 7-10   Running the JSP with the ID parameter ALFKI.

Silverlight and ASP.NET

ASP.NET is a powerful and flexible framework that is used for building everything from enterprise class, scalable applications to smaller personal home pages. It's also a terrific framework for building compelling and dynamic Silverlight applications. In this section, we'll look at three uses of ASP.NET for building Silverlight applications. The first is inline ASP.NET code (similar to PHP and JSP), in which you enhance your HTML code with logic written using a .NET framework language. Then, we'll examine how to build an ASP.NET application that uses the code-behind model to consume a Web service and deliver its results as XAML.

Finally, we'll look at how you can build ASP.NET Web services that deliver a XAML payload, and how AJAX can be used in the client to consume them.

Using Silverlight in an ASP.NET Page

ASP.NET Pages (also known as Web Forms) can work in a way that is very similar to what we saw earlier with PHP and JSP to emit HTML code marked up with source code that will execute as the page is being processed. It also provides a code-behind model in which code can be separated from the markup.

In this first example, we'll use the inline code method to show a simple ASP.NET page dynamic XAML delivery. You can see the application in Figure 7-11. The query string takes a single parameter, *Color*, and fills the handsome fellow's nose with that color. Figure 7-11 shows the result of specifying the *Color* parameter as *White*.

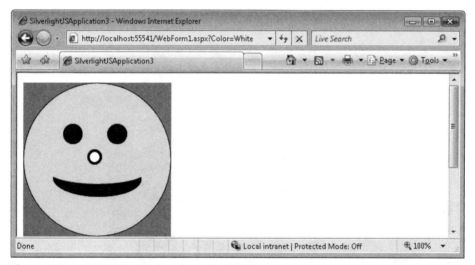

Figure 7-11 ASP.NET providing dynamic XAML.

The code for this application is shown in Listing 7-5. It uses inline XAML within a *Script* block with the ID *xamlSource*. In the *createSilverlight* function, you then provide the *source* property with the string "#xamlSource" to indicate the use of this *Script* block.

Listing 7-5 ASP.NET Dynamic Silverlight Page

```
<%@ Page Language="C#" AutoEventWireup="true" %>

<!DOCTYPE html PUBLIC "-//W3C//DTD XHTML 1.0 Transitional//EN" "http://www.w3.org/TR/
xhtml1/DTD/xhtml1-transitional.dtd">

<html xmlns="http://www.w3.org/1999/xhtml">
<head>
    <% String strColor = "";
       if( Request.Params["Color"] != null)
```

```
              strColor = Request.Params["Color"];
          else
              strColor = "Red";
      %>    <title>SilverlightJSApplication3</title>

    <script type="text/javascript" src="Silverlight.js"></script>
    <script type="text/javascript" src="createSilverlight.js"></script>
    <script type="text/xaml" id="xamlSource"><?xml version='1.0' ?>
    <Canvas xmlns='http://schemas.microsoft.com/client/2007'
            xmlns:x='http://schemas.microsoft.com/winfx/2006/xaml'
            Width='240' Height='240' Background='#FFBA9696'>
        <Ellipse Fill='#FFEAF039' Stroke='#FF000000' Width='240' Height='240'/>
        <Ellipse Fill='#FF000000' Stroke='#FF000000' Width='32' Height='32'
            Canvas.Left='64' Canvas.Top='64'/>
        <Ellipse Fill='#FF000000' Stroke='#FF000000' Width='32' Height='32'
            Canvas.Left='136' Canvas.Top='64'/>
            <Ellipse RenderTransformOrigin='0.5,0.5' Fill='#FF000000'
                Stroke='#FF000000' StrokeThickness='0'
                Width='144' Height='55.998' Canvas.Left='48'
                Canvas.Top='122.002'>
            <Ellipse.RenderTransform>
                <TransformGroup>
                    <ScaleTransform ScaleX='1' ScaleY='1'/>
                    <SkewTransform AngleX='0' AngleY='0'/>
                    <RotateTransform Angle='0.796'/>
                    <TranslateTransform X='0' Y='0'/>
                </TransformGroup>
            </Ellipse.RenderTransform>
        </Ellipse>
        <Ellipse Fill='#FFEAF039' Stroke='#FF000000'
            StrokeThickness='0' Width='160' Height='40'
            Canvas.Left='40' Canvas.Top='118'/>
        <Ellipse Fill='<% Response.Write(strColor); %>' Stroke='#FF000000'
            Width='24' Height='24' Canvas.Left='104' Canvas.Top='104'
            RenderTransformOrigin='-0.75,1.75' StrokeThickness='4'/>
    </Canvas>
</script>
</head>
<body>
    <div id="SilverlightControlHost">
        <script type="text/javascript">
            createSilverlight();
        </script>
    </div>
</body>
</html>
```

The first block of ASP.NET code (between <% and %>) is standard to every ASP.NET page. It is the page directive and serves to control ASP.NET's interaction with the page. The second ASP.NET script block extracts the *Color* parameter from the *HTTPRequest*, and if it isn't provided, the color defaults to *Red*. Note that the color value is maintained in the *strColor* variable. Then, as part of issuing the XAML for the smiley face in the final script block, the ASP.NET processor works its magic with the last *Ellipse* and records *strColor* in the ellipse's *Fill* property. The end result—if you use a XAML named color as the *Color* parameter value—fills the character's nose with that color.

Generating XAML from a Template in the Code-Behind Source

Part of the strength of ASP.NET is that it allows you to build enterprise applications using the code-behind programming model, and one advantage of this is that it permits easy consumption of Web services. This example demonstrates a simple approach to consuming Web services using a synchronous model. Keep in mind that, in general, this is not recommended for production systems—instead, consider using asynchronous pages so that the server thread pool is used more optimally.

In this next example, you'll look at consuming a server-side Web service that provides detailed stock quote information. You'll use this quote information when you generate XAML to be passed to a Silverlight-enabled browser. You can see the application in action in Figure 7-12.

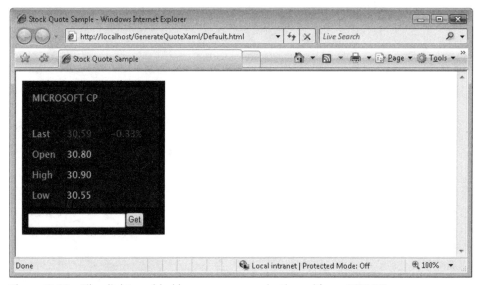

Figure 7-12   Silverlight-enabled browser communicating with an ASP.NET server.

The workhorse of this application is an ASP.NET Web Form that generates the XAML in response to a request containing a parameter with the stock symbol for which the user wants a quote. The ASP.NET form references a public Web service, retrieves the quote details, and then uses them when creating a XAML template for display. You can see the XAML template for this UI in Listing 7-6.

Listing 7-6   Stock Quote XAML Template

```
<Canvas
  xmlns="http://schemas.microsoft.com/winfx/2006/xaml/presentation"
  xmlns:x="http://schemas.microsoft.com/winfx/2006/xaml"
  Width="232" Height="308"
  Background="#FF232222"
  >
  <TextBlock Width="168" Height="24" Canvas.Left="16" Canvas.Top="16"
    Foreground="#FFCCB5B5" TextWrapping="Wrap" x:Name="tTitle"/>
  <TextBlock Width="48" Height="24" Foreground="#FFCCB5B5" Text="Last"
    TextWrapping="Wrap" Canvas.Left="16" Canvas.Top="72"/>
  <TextBlock Width="56" Height="24" Foreground="#FF00FF50" TextWrapping="Wrap"
    Canvas.Top="72" x:Name="tLast" Canvas.Left="72">28.89</TextBlock>
  <TextBlock Width="48" Height="24" Foreground="#FFCCB5B5" TextWrapping="Wrap"
    Canvas.Top="104" Canvas.Left="16">Open</TextBlock>
  <TextBlock Width="48" Height="24" Foreground="#FFCCB5B5" Text="High"
    TextWrapping="Wrap" Canvas.Top="136" Canvas.Left="16"/>
  <TextBlock Width="48" Height="24" Foreground="#FFCCB5B5" Text="Low"
    TextWrapping="Wrap" Canvas.Top="168" Canvas.Left="16"/>
  <TextBlock Width="56" Height="24" Foreground="#FFCBF100" TextWrapping="Wrap"
    Canvas.Top="104" x:Name="tOpen" Canvas.Left="72">28.89</TextBlock>
  <TextBlock Width="56" Height="24" Foreground="#FFCBF100" TextWrapping="Wrap"
    Canvas.Top="136" x:Name="tHigh" Canvas.Left="72">28.89</TextBlock>
  <TextBlock Width="56" Height="24" Foreground="#FFCBF100" TextWrapping="Wrap"
    Canvas.Top="168" x:Name="tLow" Canvas.Left="72">28.89</TextBlock>
  <TextBlock Width="64" Height="24" Foreground="#FF00FF50" TextWrapping="Wrap"
    Canvas.Top="72" Canvas.Left="144" x:Name="tChange" />
  <Rectangle Fill="#13FFFFFF" Stroke="#FF000000" StrokeThickness="2" RadiusX="2"
    RadiusY="2" Width="216" Height="192" Canvas.Left="8" Canvas.Top="8"/>
</Canvas>
```

Note that the *TextBlock* elements are named, and we'll use these names as we locate the *TextBlock* elements in the XML document using XPath.

An ASP.NET page returns HTML markup by default, and the default ASP.NET page template as provided by Visual Studio includes such basic markup as the *HTML*, *HEAD*, *BODY*, and *FORM* tags. In this case, we want the page to return XAML that is generated in the code-behind file, so we need to delete all of the HTML markup provided by Visual Studio. However, you should keep the first line of the .aspx file, so that the page declaration is preserved and the code-behind declaration is maintained. The page code for an ASP.NET page that generates XAML should look like this:

```
<%@ Page Language="C#" AutoEventWireup="true"
    CodeFile="GenerateXAML.aspx.cs" Inherits="GenerateXAML" %>
```

The code-behind file for this page will then perform the following steps:

1. Accept the input parameter, and if it is not present, provide a default value.

2. Use the Web service proxy to call the stock quote Web service (located at *http://www.webservicex.net/stockquote.asmx*) and retrieve the results.

3. The results of the particular Web service we'll use are returned as XML, so load the result into an XML document.

4. Load the XAML template into an XML document.

5. For each of the fields that we are interested in, get the value from the quote result XML document and put it into the XAML template document.

6. Set the MIME type of the *HttpResponse* to *text/xaml* and write the contents of the XML document that was generated from the template to the output stream.

You can see the code for the *Page_Load* method that implements this algorithm in Listing 7-7.

Listing 7-7   ASP.NET Page Load Method to Generate XAML

```
protected void Page_Load(object sender, EventArgs e)
{
    // Process Parameters
    bool bUp = false;
    string strTicker;
    if (Request.QueryString["ticker"] == null)
        strTicker = "MSFT";
    else
        strTicker = Request.QueryString["ticker"].ToUpper();

    // Make Web Service Call to get Quote
    QuoteService.StockQuote myQuote = new QuoteService.StockQuote();
    string strQuote = myQuote.GetQuote(strTicker);
    XmlDocument xmlQuote = new XmlDocument();
    xmlQuote.LoadXml(strQuote);

    System.Xml.XmlDocument xmlDoc = new XmlDocument();
    xmlDoc.Load(Server.MapPath("template.xaml"));

    NameTable myn = new NameTable();
    XmlNamespaceManager mng = new XmlNamespaceManager(new NameTable());
    mng.AddNamespace("d",
        "http://schemas.microsoft.com/winfx/2006/xaml/presentation");
    mng.AddNamespace("x",
        "http://schemas.microsoft.com/winfx/2006/xaml");

    XmlNode xTextBlockNode;

    // Edit the Change price
    string strChange =
        xmlQuote.SelectSingleNode("//PercentageChange").InnerText;
    if(strChange.Contains("+"))
        bUp = true;
```

```
    xTextBlockNode =
        xmlDoc.SelectSingleNode("//d:TextBlock[@x:Name='tChange']", mng);
    xTextBlockNode.InnerText =
        xmlQuote.SelectSingleNode("//PercentageChange").InnerText;
    if(!bUp)
        xTextBlockNode.Attributes["Foreground"].Value = "red";
    else
        xTextBlockNode.Attributes["Foreground"].Value = "lightgreen";

    // Edit the Company Name
    xTextBlockNode =
        xmlDoc.SelectSingleNode("//d:TextBlock[@x:Name='tTitle']", mng);
    xTextBlockNode.InnerText =
        xmlQuote.SelectSingleNode("//Name").InnerText;

    // Edit the LAST price
    xTextBlockNode =
        xmlDoc.SelectSingleNode("//d:TextBlock[@x:Name='tLast']",mng);
    xTextBlockNode.InnerText = xmlQuote.SelectSingleNode("//Last").InnerText;
    if(!bUp)
        xTextBlockNode.Attributes["Foreground"].Value = "red";
    else
        xTextBlockNode.Attributes["Foreground"].Value = "lightgreen";

    // Edit the OPEN price
    xTextBlockNode =
        xmlDoc.SelectSingleNode("//d:TextBlock[@x:Name='tOpen']", mng);
    xTextBlockNode.InnerText = xmlQuote.SelectSingleNode("//Open").InnerText;

    // Edit the HIGH price
    xTextBlockNode =
        xmlDoc.SelectSingleNode("//d:TextBlock[@x:Name='tHigh']", mng);
    xTextBlockNode.InnerText = xmlQuote.SelectSingleNode("//High").InnerText;

    // Edit the LOW price
    xTextBlockNode =
        xmlDoc.SelectSingleNode("//d:TextBlock[@x:Name='tLow']", mng);
    xTextBlockNode.InnerText = xmlQuote.SelectSingleNode("//Low").InnerText;

    // Edit the Change price
    xTextBlockNode =
        xmlDoc.SelectSingleNode("//d:TextBlock[@x:Name='tChange']", mng);
    xTextBlockNode.InnerText =
        xmlQuote.SelectSingleNode("//PercentageChange").InnerText;

    Response.ContentType = "text/xaml";
    Response.Write(xmlDoc.OuterXml);
}
```

You can see how this looks in the browser in Figure 7-13.

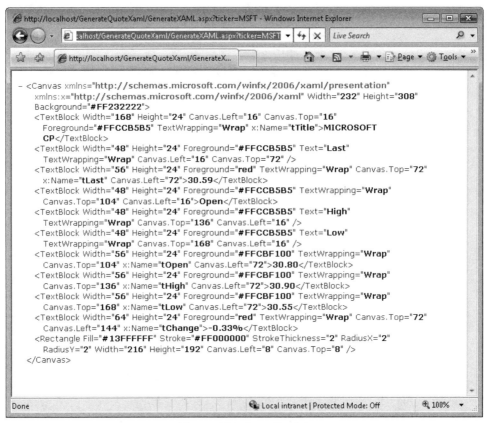

Figure 7-13 Generating XAML with an ASP.NET application.

This XAML is really meant to be consumed by a static HTML page that uses a Silverlight control. We'll create the page so that the Silverlight control is in windowless mode, allowing us to overlay the HTML text box and button, as you can see in Figure 7-12. When the user provides a stock symbol and clicks the Go button, a JavaScript function accepts the text they have entered and creates a URL query string for the stock quote generation service. The JavaScript code then sets the *source* of the Silverlight control to this URL, and when the XAML result is available, the control will rerender itself. The JavaScript code that achieves this follows:

```
<script type="text/javascript">
   function Button1_onclick() {
      var slControl = document.getElementById("AgControl1");
      var ticker = document.getElementById("Text1").value;
      slControl.Source = "GenerateXaml.aspx?ticker=" + ticker;
   }
</script>
```

The end result is a Silverlight application that accepts dynamically generated XAML from an ASP.NET server (that in turn retrieves the dynamic information from a distant Web service).

In the next section, you'll see another use case that will show you how ASP.NET, ASP.NET AJAX, and Silverlight can be used together to build another dynamic application.

Silverlight, ASP.NET, and ASP.NET AJAX

The ASP.NET AJAX extensions are very useful and powerful, because they can provide you with the power to build HTML and JavaScript applications that can consume Web services directly from the client. This is useful for building Silverlight applications that use JavaScript for their programming logic as well. In this case study, you'll see how you can build an ASP.NET Web service that is consumed by the AJAX libraries and exposed to a Silverlight presentation tier.

Building the Web Service

In order for an ASP.NET Web service to be consumable by an ASP.NET AJAX JavaScript proxy, it has to be built as a scriptable service. In this case, the Web service will provide a Web method that returns the names of all the customers in the Northwind database that match a particular country. It is built as a scriptable Web service using the *System.Web.Script.Services* namespace, and it will be decorated with the *ScriptService* attribute.

The Web service will query the database and will receive a set of customer names in return. It will use this set of names as it generates XAML containing a *TextBlock* element for each customer. The XAML will be consumed by a Silverlight control on the client. Listing 7-8 has the complete code for this Web service.

Listing 7-8   Web Service That Generates XAML

```
using System;
using System.Web;
using System.Collections;
using System.Web.Services;
using System.Web.Services.Protocols;
using System.Data;
using System.Data.SqlClient;
using System.Web.Script.Services;
using System.Text;
using System.Configuration;

/// <summary>
/// Summary description for DataService
/// </summary>
[WebService(Namespace = "http://tempuri.org/")]
[WebServiceBinding(ConformsTo = WsiProfiles.BasicProfile1_1)]
[ScriptService]
public class DataService : System.Web.Services.WebService {

    public DataService () {
    }
```

```
[WebMethod]
public string getCustomerDetails(string strCountry)
{
    int nCanvasTop = 0;
    StringBuilder strReturn = new StringBuilder();
    strReturn.Append("<Canvas>");
    SqlConnection sqlCon = null;
    try
    {
        string strConnectionString = (string)ConfigurationManager.
                    ConnectionStrings["MyNorthwind"].ConnectionString;
        sqlCon = new SqlConnection(strConnectionString);
        SqlCommand sqlComm = new SqlCommand();
        sqlComm.Connection = sqlCon;
        sqlComm.CommandType = CommandType.Text;
        sqlComm.CommandText =
          "SELECT ContactName FROM dbo.Customers WHERE (Country = @strCC)";
        sqlComm.Parameters.Add(new SqlParameter("@strCC", strCountry));
        sqlCon.Open();
        SqlDataReader sRead = sqlComm.ExecuteReader();
        while (sRead.Read())
        {
            strReturn.AppendFormat("<TextBlock Canvas.Top='{0}' " +
                            "Foreground='White' Text='{1}' />",
                            nCanvasTop, sRead["ContactName"]);
            nCanvasTop += 20;
        }
    }
    catch
    {
        // Clear what's there
        strReturn = new StringBuilder();
        strReturn.Append("<Canvas>");
    }
    finally
    {
        // Close the canvas element
        strReturn.Append("</Canvas>");

        // Close the connection
        if (sqlCon != null) sqlCon.Close();
    }

    return strReturn.ToString();
}
}
```

Executing this Web service will return a string containing a XAML block. You can see an example of this, rendered by the browser, in Figure 7-14.

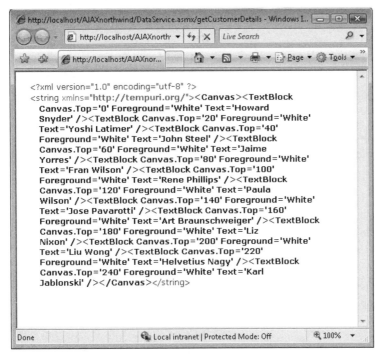

Figure 7-14   Viewing the XAML generated by the Web service.

Now let's turn to the task of displaying the XAML we've just generated. ASP.NET AJAX provides a *ScriptManager* component that is used to deliver scripts to the browser that support AJAX, as well as any other scripts. This can be used to deliver the Silverlight scripts, and when you combine Silverlight and ASP.NET AJAX, it is recommended that you use *ScriptManager* to make sure that the Silverlight scripts are delivered to the browser in the correct order. You can also use *ScriptManager* to create a reference to any scriptable Web services, allowing the *ScriptManager* to download and include the JavaScript proxy that represents the scriptable Web service.

The Web page that hosts Silverlight will accept the country parameter and will use that when it invokes the XAML-generation Web service. Following is the JavaScript that the ASP.NET page will host. Note the embedded ASP.NET markup that writes the contents of the parameter to the resulting page HTML:

```
<script type="text/javascript">
    var strCC ='<%
        string strCountry;
        if (Request.QueryString["country"] == null)
            strCountry = "Germany";
        else
            strCountry = Request.QueryString["country"].ToUpper();
        Response.Write(strCountry);
    %>';
    var m_Control;
```

```
    var m_RootElement;
</script>
```

When the page is called with the parameter *Country=Germany*, the HTML/JavaScript that the browser will render looks like this:

```
<script type="text/javascript">
    var strCC ='Germany';
    var m_Control;
    var m_RootElement;
</script>
```

The JavaScript Web service proxy allows you to access the Web service. This object has the same name as the Web service, so to access it from JavaScript, you simply call the Web method exposed by this object. This is done in the *handleLoad* function. Note that the page-global variables *m_Control* and *m_RootElement* are set to the *control* and *rootElement* parameters that the *handleLoad* event receives. These will be needed a little later, so we'll capture them now.

Following is the *handleLoad* code:

```
function handleLoad(control, userContext, rootElement)
{
    m_Control=control;
    m_RootElement=rootElement;
    DataService.getCustomerDetails(strCC, onReturn, onTimeout);
}
```

When calling a Web service in JavaScript, you specify the callback functions for a successful return and a failed or timed-out invocation. So, when the service succeeds and returns the XAML block as outlined earlier, it will be passed to the callback function *onReturn*. (Conversely, when it fails, *onTimeout* will be called.)

In this case, the callback function can use *createFromXaml* to add the XAML to the Silverlight control and thus render it. Here is the code:

```
function onReturn(result)
{
    // Define a XAML fragment and create it.
    var xamlFragment = result;
    textBlock = m_Control.content.createFromXaml(xamlFragment);

    // Add the XAML fragment as a child of the root Canvas object.
    m_RootElement.children.add(textBlock);
}
```

The complete listing for the ASP.NET page containing Silverlight and AJAX is shown in Listing 7-9.

Listing 7-9   AJAX, Silverlight, and ASP.NET

```
<%@ Page Language="C#" AutoEventWireup="true" CodeFile="Default.aspx.cs"
Inherits="_Default" %>

<!DOCTYPE html PUBLIC "-//W3C//DTD XHTML 1.1//EN" "http://www.w3.org/TR/xhtml11/DTD/
xhtml11.dtd">
<html xmlns="http://www.w3.org/1999/xhtml">
<head runat="server">
    <title>AJAX and Silverlight</title>
    <script type="text/javascript">
      var strCC ='<%
          string strCountry;
          if (Request.QueryString["Country"] == null)
              strCountry = "Germany";
          else
              strCountry = Request.QueryString["Country"].ToUpper();
          Response.Write(strCountry);
      %>';
      var m_Control;
      var m_RootElement;
    </script>

</head>
<body>
    <form id="form1" runat="server">
        <asp:ScriptManager ID="ScriptManager1" runat="server">
            <Services>
                <asp:ServiceReference Path="~/DataService.asmx" />
            </Services>
            <Scripts>
                <asp:ScriptReference Path="Silverlight.js" />
                <asp:ScriptReference Path="createSilverlight.js" />
            </Scripts>
        </asp:ScriptManager>

        <script type="text/javascript">
          function handleLoad(control, userContext, rootElement)
          {
              m_Control=control;
              m_RootElement=rootElement;
              DataService.getCustomerDetails(strCC, onReturn, onTimeout);
          }
          function onReturn(result)
          {
              // Define a XAML fragment and create it.
              var xamlFragment = result;
              textBlock = m_Control.content.createFromXaml(xamlFragment);

              // Add the XAML fragment as a child of the root Canvas object.
              m_RootElement.children.add(textBlock);
          }
          function onTimeout(result)
          {
          }
```

```
        </script>
        <div id="SilverlightControlHost">
            <script type="text/javascript">
                createSilverlight();
            </script>
        </div>
    </form>
</body>
</html>
```

When you run this page and pass it the name of a country as the parameter, it will then render the customer names from the Northwind database for the customer data matching that country. Figure 7-15 shows a list of names that would display if you ran the page with *Country=USA*.

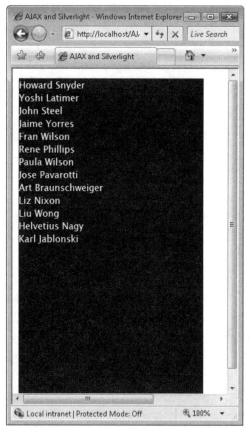

Figure 7-15   Calling the AJAX Page with the parameter Country=USA.

Summary

In this chapter, you saw how Silverlight can be delivered from various server technologies that enable dynamic XAML generation. You were introduced to PHP and learned how simple it is to use PHP to generate templated XAML, which can be integrated with ease into a Silverlight-enabled browser. You saw how various Java-based technologies such as servlets and JSP pages can also be used to build data-driven, dynamic Silverlight sites.

Finally, you looked at ASP.NET, and saw several examples in which it could be used to build applications that use Silverlight. You saw how ASP.NET can consume server-side databases or Web services and turn the resulting data into XAML, how page-level markup can write template XAML to an output stream, and how—together with AJAX and scriptable services—you can put together dynamic user interfaces.

The next chapter offers you a preview of the future of Silverlight and the features it supports, such as the embedded .NET Framework code, the new Silverlight controls, and the new ASP.NET controls that you can use to build Silverlight applications when developing applications using Visual Studio 2008.

Chapter 8
Silverlight Futures

Microsoft has been very open about their plans for Silverlight, including providing a developer preview of Silverlight 1.1 Alpha and the ASP.NET Futures toolkit that includes Silverlight support. In this chapter, we offer a high-level look at some of the features of Silverlight 1.1. You'll get some hands-on experience with an early version of the framework and the code, which will provide you with a head start in developing with it as well as a better understanding of Silverlight as it evolves.

What Is Silverlight 1.1?

Silverlight 1.1 adds .NET development, which will allow you to use VB and C# code in your rich interactive Internet applications. In addition, Silverlight's Dynamic Language Runtime (DLR) provides facilities for Dynamic Languages such as Python and Ruby to your toolbox. If you aren't familiar with Dynamic Languages, these are high-level programming languages that are interpreted and execute at run time, and provide run time extensibility to your program. For example, they might allow you to extend objects or create functions while the code is executing. Silverlight 1.1 also brings an extended set of controls and namespaces for your development. These include XML processing, a network protocol stack, isolated and protected storage, and more. These extensions can be seen in Figure 8-1.

Getting Started with Silverlight 1.1

Before you start coding with Silverlight 1.1, you will need to download the following software:

- Microsoft Visual Studio 2008
- Microsoft Silverlight Tools for Visual Studio 2008
- Expression Blend 2 Preview
- Microsoft Silverlight 1.1 Software Development Kit
- Microsoft ASP.NET Futures

You can find a link to each of these tools from the Silverlight community site at *http://www.silverlight.net*.

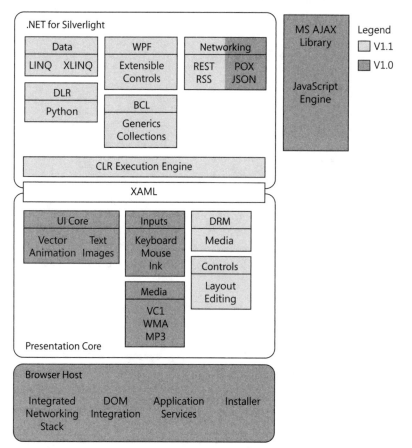

Figure 8-1   Silverlight 1.1 architecture.

Note   All of the examples in this chapter were built using Visual Studio 2008, Beta 2 (code name Orcas). Because this was very much a work in progress at time of publication, you may notice some minor changes from the version used in this book. If you get stuck, be sure to look for the latest quick starts and guides at *http://www.silverlight.net* and *http://www.asp.net*.

When the Silverlight tools for Visual Studio 2008 are installed, you'll see a new template for Silverlight in the New Project dialog box. This allows you to create a Silverlight project or a Silverlight class library, as shown in Figure 8-2.

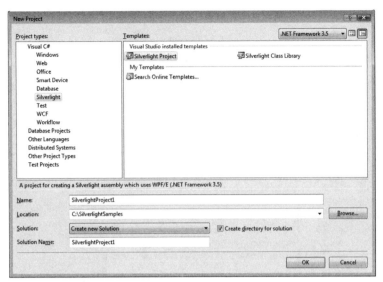

Figure 8-2   Silverlight project templates in Visual Studio.

When you create a new Silverlight project, you'll see a project directory setup similar to what you're familiar with in Silverlight 1.0. You'll have a Default.html file containing the Silverlight control as well as its code-behind Default.html.js JavaScript file. In addition, the project will contain a default XAML page called Page.xaml as well as its C# code-behind file, Page.xaml.cs.

The XAML will contain references to the compiled assembly or assemblies that the Silverlight project requires. Following is an example:

```
<Canvas x:Name="parentCanvas"
        xmlns="http://schemas.microsoft.com/client/2007"
        xmlns:x="http://schemas.microsoft.com/winfx/2006/xaml"
        Loaded="Page_Loaded"
        x:Class="SilverlightProject1Page;assembly=ClientBin/Chapter8Example1.dll"
        Width="640"
        Height="480"
        Background="White"
        >
```

You can see that the *x:Class* attribute has been added; this defines the name of the class within the assembly that Visual Studio will create for you when this project is compiled as well as the assembly location.

With this assembly, instead of writing event handlers in JavaScript, you can write them in C#, VB, or any of the other languages that are supported by the DLR. The resulting code will be in the class indicated by the *x:Class* attribute.

Let's take a look at a simple example. In this example, the XAML contains eight text blocks. At run time, you are going to bind an event hander to the *MouseEnter* and *MouseLeave* events to change the text of these text blocks as the mouse passes over them.

Following is the XAML for the example project "SilverlightProject1":

```
<Canvas x:Name="parentCanvas"
        xmlns="http://schemas.microsoft.com/client/2007"
        xmlns:x="http://schemas.microsoft.com/winfx/2006/xaml"
        Loaded="Page_Loaded"
        x:Class="SilverlightProject1.Page;assembly=ClientBin/Chapter8Example1.dll"
        Width="640"
        Height="480"
        Background="White"
        >
  <TextBlock Canvas.Top="0" Foreground="Black" Text="TextBlock 1" />
  <TextBlock Canvas.Top="20" Foreground="Black" Text="TextBlock 2" />
  <TextBlock Canvas.Top="40" Foreground="Black" Text="TextBlock 3" />
  <TextBlock Canvas.Top="60" Foreground="Black" Text="TextBlock 4" />
  <TextBlock Canvas.Top="80" Foreground="Black" Text="TextBlock 5" />
  <TextBlock Canvas.Top="100" Foreground="Black" Text="TextBlock 6" />
  <TextBlock Canvas.Top="120" Foreground="Black" Text="TextBlock 7" />
  <TextBlock Canvas.Top="140" Foreground="Black" Text="TextBlock 8" />
</Canvas>
```

Note that the *Canvas* element defines a *Page_Loaded* event to handle the *Canvas* loaded event. You can see how this is used in C#:

```
public void Page_Loaded(object o, EventArgs e)
{
    // Required to initialize variables
    InitializeComponent();

    foreach (TextBlock tt in this.Children)
    {
        tt.MouseEnter += new MouseEventHandler(OnEnter);
        tt.MouseLeave += new EventHandler(OnLeave);
    }
}
```

Here, the C# code loops through each *TextBlock* in the *Canvas* and assigns event handler functions to their *MouseEnter* and *MouseLeave* events. These are called *OnEnter* and *OnLeave* respectively. Following is the code for *OnEnter*:

```
public void OnEnter(object sender, MouseEventArgs e)
{
    TextBlock tt = sender as TextBlock;
    strCurrentText = tt.Text;
    tt.Text = "I am in : " + strCurrentText;
}
```

The variable *strCurrentText* is a class variable, shared between each of these helper functions. So, when you enter any of *TextBlock* controls, the value of its *Text* property is copied into this variable. From there, the *Text* property is changed to read "I am in : " followed by the original name.

When you leave the *TextBlock*, you'll need to reset the original text. Here is the code that does that:

```
public void OnLeave(object sender, EventArgs e)
{
    TextBlock tt = sender as TextBlock;
    tt.Text = strCurrentText;
}
```

Now when you run the application, you get a mouse "hot track" as it travels over the *TextBlock* controls. You see this in Figure 8-3.

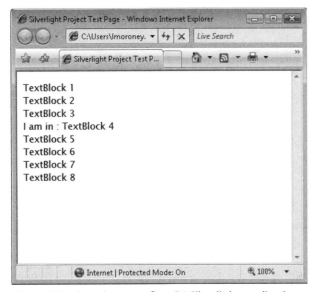

Figure 8-3 Running your first C# Silverlight application.

Building a Custom Control in Silverlight 1.1

Silverlight 1.1 adds the ability to build custom controls and integrate them into your XAML while maintaining their application logic executing within .NET. In this section, you'll work through a simple example of a custom control that draws a circle.

Creating the Control Project

To get started, use Visual Studio Orcas to create a new Silverlight class library. You can do this by selecting Silverlight as a project type and the Silverlight Class Library template as the template type in the New Project dialog box, as shown in Figure 8-4.

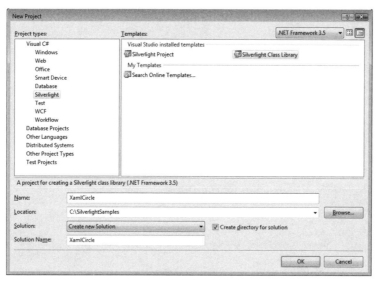

Figure 8-4   Creating a new Silverlight control class library.

By doing this, you will create a Silverlight class library that contains the appropriate references for a Silverlight 1.1 application and a class called *Class1* in the Class1.cs file. You can see the project in Solution Explorer in Figure 8-5.

Figure 8-5   An example Silverlight class library project.

The first thing you need to do is to delete the Class1.cs file, because this file is not going to be used in this sample. Then, right-click the project name (*XamlCircle*), select Add from the short-cut menu, and then select New Item. You can see the menus in Figure 8-6.

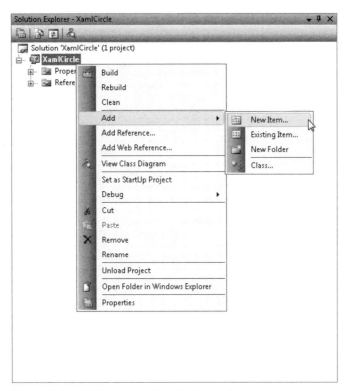

Figure 8-6   Adding a new item to the project.

This will launch the Add New Item dialog box, which you can use to add new items. We're going to build a new Silverlight user control, so select the Silverlight User Control template, as you can see in Figure 8-7. Make sure that you name the file Circle.xaml so that it matches the code in the rest of this section.

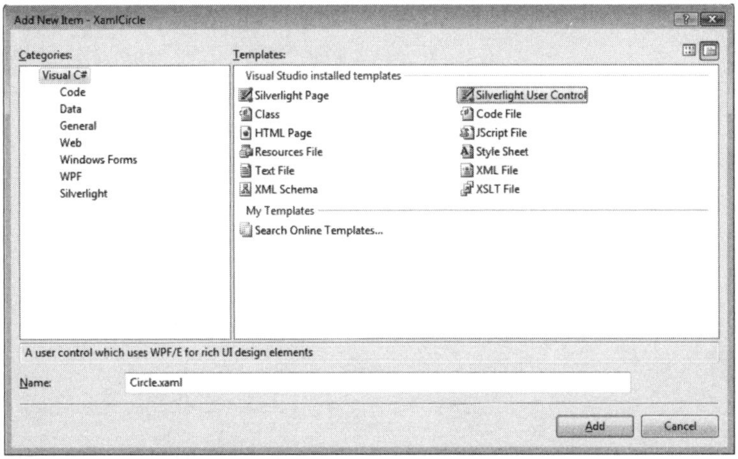

Figure 8-7   Adding a new Silverlight user control.

You'll notice that two new files are added to your project—Circle.xaml and its associated code-behind file, Circle.xaml.cs. If you look at the Circle.xaml file, you should see this XAML code:

```
<Canvas xmlns="http://schemas.microsoft.com/client/2007"
        xmlns:x="http://schemas.microsoft.com/winfx/2006/xaml"
        Width="640"
        Height="480"
        Background="White"
        >

</Canvas>
```

As you can see, the XAML code consists of a containing *Canvas*, nothing else. This *Canvas* is used as the bounds of your control, and you define the XAML for the inner elements as children of this *Canvas*. Because our control is very simple—just a circle—it will contain only one child element—an ellipse. Please note that this is an extremely simple example, but you aren't limited to simple controls like this—full XAML, including other controls, animations, timelines, and so forth, may be used in custom controls. Note also that any controls that you are going to be exposing should be named. Following is the XAML containing the ellipse:

```
<Canvas xmlns="http://schemas.microsoft.com/client/2007"
        xmlns:x="http://schemas.microsoft.com/winfx/2006/xaml"
        Width="640"
        Height="480"
        Background="White"
        >
  <Ellipse x:Name="circle"></Ellipse>
</Canvas>
```

Writing the Control Code

The default code-behind file contains a constructor that reads the XAML and instantiates the *FrameWorkElement*-based control:

```
public Circle()
{
    System.IO.Stream s =
      this.GetType().Assembly.GetManifestResourceStream("XamlCircle.Circle.xaml");
    this.InitializeFromXaml(new System.IO.StreamReader(s).ReadToEnd());
}
```

Let's now edit this code to expose the ellipse element. The full listing is shown in Listing 8-1.

Listing 8-1   Code-Behind for Circle Control

```
using System;
using System.Windows;
using System.Windows.Controls;
using System.Windows.Documents;
using System.Windows.Ink;
using System.Windows.Input;
using System.Windows.Media;
using System.Windows.Media.Animation;
using System.Windows.Shapes;

namespace XamlCircle
{
    public class Circle : Control
    {
        FrameworkElement implRoot;
        Ellipse circ;
        public Circle()
        {
            System.IO.Stream s =
                    this.GetType().Assembly.
                        GetManifestResourceStream("XamlCircle.Circle.xaml");
            implRoot = this.InitializeFromXaml(new
                    System.IO.StreamReader(s).ReadToEnd());
            circ = implRoot.FindName("circle") as Ellipse;
            this.Loaded += new EventHandler(Circle_Loaded);
            base.Width = implRoot.Width;
            base.Height = implRoot.Height;
        }

        void Circle_Loaded(object sender, EventArgs e)
        {
            UpdateLayout();
        }

        public double Radius
        {
            get
            {
                return circ.Width / 2;

            }
            set
            {
                circ.Width = value * 2;
                circ.Height = value * 2;
                UpdateLayout();
            }
        }

        public SolidColorBrush FillColor
        {
            get
            {
```

```
                    return (SolidColorBrush)circ.Fill;
            }
            set
            {
                circ.Fill = (SolidColorBrush)value;
            }
        }

        protected void UpdateLayout()
        {
            implRoot.Width = circ.Width;
            implRoot.Height = circ.Height;
        }
    }
}
```

This code sets up global variables for the *FrameWorkElement*, called *implRoot*, and the inner *Ellipse* that will render the circle, called *circ*. The constructor has also been modified to assign the result of the default constructor code that read the XAML and to assign the results of the *initializefromXAML* method to the *implRoot* variable. It then uses *findFromXAML* to locate the ellipse and assigns a reference to it using the *circ* variable. Finally, the code hooks the *Loaded* event and then initializes the control's dimensions.

When the control is loaded, the *Circle_Loaded* function is called. (This was hooked in the constructor.) This function in turn calls the *UpdateLayout* method, which we'll see in a moment. Following is the code for *Circle_Loaded*:

```
void Circle_Loaded(object sender, EventArgs e)
{
    UpdateLayout();
}
```

The *UpdateLayout* method resizes the canvas to fit the circle by matching its width and height properties to those of the circle. You can see that code here:

```
protected void UpdateLayout()
{
    implRoot.Width = circ.Width;
    implRoot.Height = circ.Height;
}
```

The *Circle* element has a *Radius* property. The underlying ellipse has *Height* and *Width* properties. In order to make this element a circle, the height and width should be twice the radius. So, the property handler for the *Circle* control's *Radius* property makes sure that these rules are followed. Following is the code for the *Radius* property:

```
public double Radius
{
    get
    {
```

```
        return circ.Width / 2;

    }
    set
    {
        circ.Width = value * 2;
        circ.Height = value * 2;
        UpdateLayout();
    }
}
```

When you retrieve the property's value, you receive half of the circle's width. When you set the property's value, you assign the height and width to twice the radius, as discussed. After the *Radius* has been set, then the *UpdateLayout* function resizes the control.

Compiling and Testing the Control

When the control is compiled, it will be built as a DLL in the *ClientBin* subdirectory. Note that this will not be added automatically to the project explorer in Visual Studio even though it will exist within the project's subdirectory on your hard drive.

To test this control, you'll need a standard Silverlight project. The easiest way to accomplish this is to create a dummy Silverlight project and then take the relevant files from it. So, follow the steps from the "Getting Started with Silverlight 1.1" section earlier in this chapter and create a dummy solution. Then, from the XamlCircle project, use the menu commands to add an existing item (refer to Figure 8-6) and select the following files from the dummy project that you just created:

- Page.xaml
- Silverlight.js
- TestPage.html
- TestPage.html.js

The default Page.xaml created by the template contains a declaration for the *Loaded* event and for the class that implements this event as assigned using the *x:Class* attribute. These should be deleted. You also need to specify the namespace of the custom control. When you've finished, the *Canvas* XAML code will look like this:

```
<Canvas x:Name="parentCanvas"
        xmlns="http://schemas.microsoft.com/client/2007"
        xmlns:x="http://schemas.microsoft.com/winfx/2006/xaml"
        xmlns:my="clr-namespace:XamlCircle;assembly=ClientBin/XamlCircle.dll"
        Width="640"
        Height="480"
        Background="White"
        >
</Canvas>
```

Note that the assembly location is *ClientBin/XamlCircle.dll*—this is where the control was compiled earlier. The *clr-namespace* attribute defines the control's namespace. If you refer back to Listing 8-1, you'll see that the *Circle* control's namespace is *XamlCircle*.

Now that we have completed the preliminary work, it's time to render the circle. To do this, we simply add the *my:Circle* element to the XAML code. Following is an example:

```
<my:Circle Radius="20" FillColor="Blue"></my:Circle>
```

Here's an example of a XAML document containing several circles:

```
<Canvas x:Name="parentCanvas"
        xmlns="http://schemas.microsoft.com/client/2007"
        xmlns:x="http://schemas.microsoft.com/winfx/2006/xaml"
        xmlns:my="clr-namespace:XamlCircle;assembly=ClientBin/XamlCircle.dll"
        Width="640"
        Height="480"
        Background="White"
        >

<my:Circle Canvas.Top="0" Canvas.Left="0"
    FillColor="Red" Radius="20"></my:Circle>
<my:Circle Canvas.Top="40" Canvas.Left="0"
    FillColor="Orange" Radius="20"></my:Circle>
<my:Circle Canvas.Top="80" Canvas.Left="0"
    FillColor="Yellow" Radius="20"></my:Circle>
<my:Circle Canvas.Top="0" Canvas.Left="40"
    FillColor="Green" Radius="20"></my:Circle>
<my:Circle Canvas.Top="40" Canvas.Left="40"
    FillColor="Blue" Radius="20"></my:Circle>
<my:Circle Canvas.Top="80" Canvas.Left="40"
    FillColor="Indigo" Radius="20"></my:Circle>
</Canvas>
```

You can see how this appears in Figure 8-8.

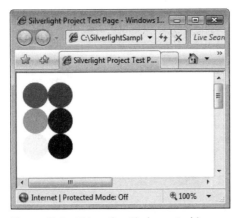

Figure 8-8 Using the *Circle* control in a page.

Using ASP.NET with Silverlight 1.1

The ASP.NET Silverlight Futures pack contains templates that allow you to use Silverlight and your custom controls in ASP.NET Web applications. It uses the simple drag-and-drop interface that you've come to expect from ASP.NET with a XAML server control that takes care of generating the markup to instantiate Silverlight on your page.

To see how this works, let's add a new ASP.NET Web application to the *Circle* control solution. First, right-click the solution, and then use the menu commands to add a new Web site, as shown in Figure 8-9.

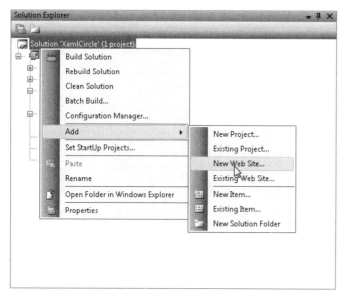

Figure 8-9   Adding a new Web site to your solution.

This will open the Add New Web Site dialog box, which allows you to select the Web site type. Select a simple ASP.NET Web site and give it a name. See Figure 8-10.

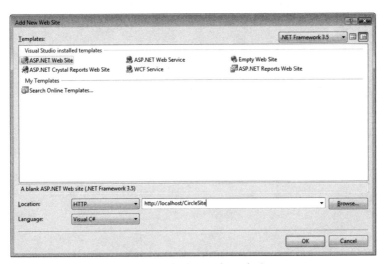

Figure 8-10 Adding a new Web site to the solution.

Now you'll have a new ASP.NET Web site in your solution that contains the basic Default.aspx page. You can connect this to your Silverlight content using the Add Silverlight Link option. To do this, right-click on the Web project and select Add Silverlight Link from the shortcut menu, as shown in Figure 8-11.

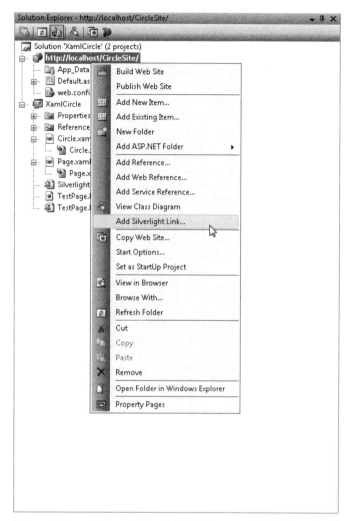

Figure 8-11 Adding a Silverlight link to your ASP.NET application.

This will open the Add Silverlight Link dialog box (Figure 8-12) that allows you to specify the Silverlight project to which you want to link. In this case, there is only one project, *XamlCircle*.

Figure 8-12   The Add Silverlight Link dialog box.

Click OK to add the dependencies for Silverlight projects to the Web site. When this is completed, Visual Studio will ask you if you want to enable Silverlight debugging. The message box is shown in Figure 8-13. This will allow you to debug the code that is running behind your Silverlight application.

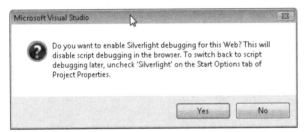

Figure 8-13   Enabling Silverlight debugging.

You can add Silverlight to the Default.aspx page using the ASP.NET XAML control. Since the Silverlight XAML server control has a dependency on the AJAX *ScriptManager* control, ASP.NET AJAX should first be added to the Default.aspx page. You can find this in Visual Studio's AJAX Extensions Toolbox section, as shown in Figure 8-14.

Figure 8-14   Adding the *ScriptManager* control to Default.aspx.

After the *ScriptManager* has been dropped onto your page, add a XAML control to the page and use the XamlURL property to reference your XAML document. Note that as you link to the XamlCircle application, you'll see that the Page.xaml, which contains some instances of the *Circle* control, is now part of the ASP.NET site. See Figure 8-15.

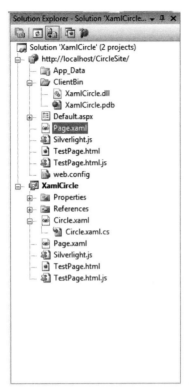

Figure 8-15   Solution Explorer when ASP.NET and Silverlight projects are linked.

The ASP.NET Futures contain a *Xaml* control, which you can drag onto the designer. Assign its *XamlUrl* property to be Page.xaml. See Figure 8-16.

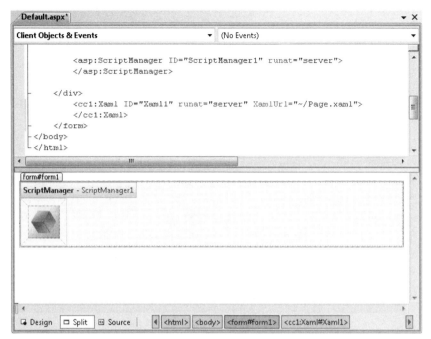

Figure 8-16   Adding XAML to the Visual Studio Web page designer.

Now, if you run the application and view the ASP.NET page, you'll see results in the browser, as shown in Figure 8-17. As you would expect, this display is identical to the one you saw earlier (in Figure 8-8).

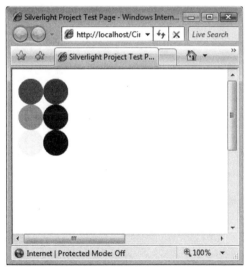

Figure 8-17   Running the ASP.NET page.

Summary

In this chapter, you were able to investigate the future of Silverlight with Silverlight 1.1 and the ASP.NET Futures control pack, and you learned that you will be able to enhance your Silverlight applications dramatically with the power of the .NET framework and .NET languages for flexibility and performance. You saw how Silverlight will work with ASP.NET and discovered the ease of building dynamic Silverlight Web sites using this technology.

At the time this was written, the information presented in this chapter was based on the early-access downloads of this new technology; the technology—and the information about how to use it—is subject to change. Even so, I hope this chapter was able to provide you with a tantalizing introduction to the exciting advances in this technology, so that you will be able to make use of it as the platform evolves. In particular, the ability to extend the Silverlight platform by building custom controls, as demonstrated in this chapter, is a skill that will undoubtedly be in great demand!

Index

Laurence Moroney

Laurence Moroney has been playing with new technologies longer than he'd care to admit. After earning a degree in physics, he realized that a better career path would be found in computing and was bitten by the programming bug some 14 years ago. He has worked on the development of applications for an extremely diverse assortment of organizations in a wide range of environments: from casinos to jails to financial services to professional sports; from Visual Basic to PHP to Java; and from embedded systems to Linux to Windows. He has filled the roles of developer, tester, architect, program manager, and all-round dogsbody, so he could be described as someone who has "been around the block." Since 2006, he has been working as a Technology Evangelist for Microsoft, where he specializes in Silverlight and the next generation Web.

Laurence's blog is at *http://blogs.msdn.com/webnext.*

Additional Resources for Web Developers

Published and Forthcoming Titles from Microsoft Press

Microsoft® Visual Web Developer™ 2005 Express Edition: Build a Web Site Now!
Jim Buyens • ISBN 0-7356-2212-4

With this lively, eye-opening, and hands-on book, all you need is a computer and the desire to learn how to create Web pages now using Visual Web Developer Express Edition! Featuring a full working edition of the software, this fun and highly visual guide walks you through a complete Web page project from set-up to launch. You'll get an introduction to the Microsoft Visual Studio® environment and learn how to put the light-weight, easy-to-use tools in Visual Web Developer Express to work right away—building your first, dynamic Web pages with Microsoft ASP.NET 2.0. You'll get expert tips, coaching, and visual examples at each step of the way, along with pointers to additional learning resources.

Microsoft ASP.NET 2.0 Programming
Step by Step
George Shepherd • ISBN 0-7356-2201-9

With dramatic improvements in performance, productivity, and security features, Visual Studio 2005 and ASP.NET 2.0 deliver a simplified, high-performance, and powerful Web development experience. ASP.NET 2.0 features a new set of controls and infrastructure that simplify Web-based data access and include functionality that facilitates code reuse, visual consistency, and aesthetic appeal. Now you can teach yourself the essentials of working with ASP.NET 2.0 in the Visual Studio environment— one step at a time. With *Step by Step*, you work at your own pace through hands-on, learn-by-doing exercises. Whether you're a beginning programmer or new to this version of the technology, you'll understand the core capabilities and fundamental techniques for ASP.NET 2.0. Each chapter puts you to work, showing you how, when, and why to use specific features of the ASP.NET 2.0 rapid application development environment and guiding you as you create actual components and working applications for the Web, including advanced features such as personalization.

Programming Microsoft ASP.NET 2.0
Core Reference
Dino Esposito • ISBN 0-7356-2176-4

Delve into the core topics for ASP.NET 2.0 programming, mastering the essential skills and capabilities needed to build high-performance Web applications successfully. Well-known ASP.NET author Dino Esposito deftly builds your expertise with Web forms, Visual Studio, core controls, master pages, data access, data binding, state management, security services, and other must-know topics—combining defini-tive reference with practical, hands-on programming instruc-tion. Packed with expert guidance and pragmatic examples, this *Core Reference* delivers the key resources that you need to develop professional-level Web programming skills.

Programming Microsoft ASP.NET 2.0
Applications: *Advanced Topics*
Dino Esposito • ISBN 0-7356-2177-2

Master advanced topics in ASP.NET 2.0 programming—gaining the essential insights and in-depth understanding that you need to build sophisticated, highly func-tional Web applications success-fully. Topics include Web forms, Visual Studio 2005, core controls, master pages, data access, data binding, state management, and security considerations. Developers often discover that the more they use ASP.NET, the more they need to know. With expert guidance from ASP.NET authority Dino Esposito, you get the in-depth, comprehensive information that leads to full mastery of the technology.

Programming Microsoft Windows® Forms
Charles Petzold • ISBN 0-7356-2153-5

Programming Microsoft Web Forms
Douglas J. Reilly • ISBN 0-7356-2179-9

CLR via C++
Jeffrey Richter with Stanley B. Lippman
ISBN 0-7356-2248-5

Debugging, Tuning, and Testing Microsoft .NET 2.0 Applications
John Robbins • ISBN 0-7356-2202-7

CLR via C#, Second Edition
Jeffrey Richter • ISBN 0-7356-2163-2

For more information about Microsoft Press® books and other learning products,
visit: **www.microsoft.com/books** *and* **www.microsoft.com/learning**

Additional Resources for Developers: Advanced Topics and Best Practices

Published and Forthcoming Titles from Microsoft Press

Code Complete, Second Edition
Steve McConnell • ISBN 0-7356-1967-0

For more than a decade, Steve McConnell, one of the premier authors and voices in the software community, has helped change the way developers write code—and produce better software. Now his classic book, *Code Complete*, has been fully updated and revised with best practices in the art and science of constructing software. Topics include design, applying good techniques to construction, eliminating errors, planning, managing construction activities, and relating personal character to superior software. This new edition features fully updated information on programming techniques, including the emergence of Web-style programming, and integrated coverage of object-oriented design. You'll also find new code examples—both good and bad—in C++, Microsoft® Visual Basic®, C#, and Java, although the focus is squarely on techniques and practices.

More About Software Requirements: Thorny Issues and Practical Advice
Karl E. Wiegers • ISBN 0-7356-2267-1

Have you ever delivered software that satisfied all of the project specifications, but failed to meet any of the customers expectations? Without formal, verifiable requirements—and a system for managing them—the result is often a gap between what developers think they're supposed to build and what customers think they're going to get. Too often, lessons about software requirements engi-
neering processes are formal or academic, and not of value to real-world, professional development teams. In this follow-up guide to *Software Requirements*, Second Edition, you will discover even more practical techniques for gathering and managing software requirements that help you deliver software that meets project and customer specifications. Succinct and immediately useful, this book is a must-have for developers and architects.

Software Estimation: Demystifying the Black Art
Steve McConnell • ISBN 0-7356-0535-1

Often referred to as the "black art" because of its complexity and uncertainty, software estimation is not as hard or mysterious as people think. However, the art of how to create effective cost and schedule estimates has not been very well publicized. *Software Estimation* provides a proven set of procedures and heuristics that software developers, technical leads, and project managers can apply to their projects. Instead of arcane treatises and rigid modeling techniques, award-winning author Steve McConnell gives practical guidance to help organizations achieve basic estimation proficiency and lay the groundwork to continue improving project cost estimates. This book does not avoid the more complex mathematical estimation approaches, but the non-mathematical reader will find plenty of useful guidelines without getting bogged down in complex formulas.

Debugging, Tuning, and Testing Microsoft .NET 2.0 Applications
John Robbins • ISBN 0-7356-2202-7

Making an application the best it can be has long been a time-consuming task best accomplished with specialized and costly tools. With Microsoft Visual Studio® 2005, developers have available a new range of built-in functionality that enables them to debug their code quickly and efficiently, tune it to op-timum performance, and test applications to ensure compat-ibility and trouble-free operation. In this accessible and hands-on book, debugging expert John Robbins shows developers how to use the tools and functions in Visual Studio to their full advantage to ensure high-quality applications.

The Security Development Lifecycle
Michael Howard and Steve Lipner • ISBN 0-7356-2214-0

Adapted from Microsoft's standard development process, the Security Development Lifecycle (SDL) is a methodology that helps reduce the number of security defects in code at every stage of the development process, from design to release. This book details each stage of the SDL methodology and discusses its implementation across a range of Microsoft software, including Microsoft Windows Server™ 2003, Microsoft SQL Server™ 2000 Service Pack 3, and Microsoft Exchange Server 2003 Service Pack 1, to help measurably improve security features. You get direct access to insights from Microsoft's security team and lessons that are applicable to software development processes worldwide, whether on a small-scale or a large-scale. This book includes a CD featuring videos of developer training classes.

Software Requirements, Second Edition
Karl E. Wiegers • ISBN 0-7356-1879-8

Writing Secure Code, Second Edition
Michael Howard and David LeBlanc • ISBN 0-7356-1722-8

CLR via C#, Second Edition
Jeffrey Richter • ISBN 0-7356-2163-2

Additional Resources for C# Developers

Published and Forthcoming Titles from Microsoft Press

Microsoft® Visual C#® 2005 Express Edition: Build a Program Now!

Patrice Pelland • ISBN 0-7356-2229-9

In this lively, eye-opening, and hands-on book, all you need is a computer and the desire to learn how to program with Visual C# 2005 Express Edition. Featuring a full working edition of the software, this fun and highly visual guide walks you through a complete programming project—a desktop weather-reporting application—from start to finish. You'll get an unintimidating introduction to the Microsoft Visual Studio® development environment and learn how to put the lightweight, easy-to-use tools in Visual C# Express to work right away—creating, compiling, testing, and delivering your first, ready-to-use program. You'll get expert tips, coaching, and visual examples at each step of the way, along with pointers to additional learning resources.

Microsoft Visual C# 2005 *Step by Step*

John Sharp • ISBN 0-7356-2129-2

Visual C#, a feature of Visual Studio 2005, is a modern programming language designed to deliver a productive environment for creating business frameworks and reusable object-oriented components. Now you can teach yourself essential techniques with Visual C#—and start building components and Microsoft Windows®–based applications—one step at a time. With *Step by Step*, you work at your own pace through hands-on, learn-by-doing exercises. Whether you're a beginning programmer or new to this particular language, you'll learn how, when, and why to use specific features of Visual C# 2005. Each chapter puts you to work, building your knowledge of core capabilities and guiding you as you create your first C#-based applications for Windows, data management, and the Web.

Programming Microsoft Visual C# 2005 Framework Reference

Francesco Balena • ISBN 0-7356-2182-9

Complementing *Programming Microsoft Visual C# 2005 Core Reference*, this book covers a wide range of additional topics and information critical to Visual C# developers, including Windows Forms, working with Microsoft ADO.NET 2.0 and Microsoft ASP.NET 2.0, Web services, security, remoting, and much more. Packed with sample code and real-world examples, this book will help developers move from understanding to mastery.

Programming Microsoft Visual C# 2005 *Core Reference*

Donis Marshall • ISBN 0-7356-2181-0

Get the in-depth reference and pragmatic, real-world insights you need to exploit the enhanced language features and core capabilities in Visual C# 2005. Programming expert Donis Marshall deftly builds your proficiency with classes, structs, and other fundamentals, and advances your expertise with more advanced topics such as debugging, threading, and memory management. Combining incisive reference with hands-on coding examples and best practices, this *Core Reference* focuses on mastering the C# skills you need to build innovative solutions for smart clients and the Web.

CLR via C#, Second Edition

Jeffrey Richter • ISBN 0-7356-2163-2

In this new edition of Jeffrey Richter's popular book, you get focused, pragmatic guidance on how to exploit the common language runtime (CLR) functionality in Microsoft .NET Framework 2.0 for applications of all types—from Web Forms, Windows Forms, and Web services to solutions for Microsoft SQL Server™, Microsoft code names "Avalon" and "Indigo," consoles, Microsoft Windows NT® Service, and more. Targeted to advanced developers and software designers, this book takes you under the covers of .NET for an in-depth understanding of its structure, functions, and operational components, demonstrating the most practical ways to apply this knowledge to your own development efforts. You'll master fundamental design tenets for .NET and get hands-on insights for creating high-performance applications more easily and efficiently. The book features extensive code examples in Visual C# 2005.

Programming Microsoft Windows Forms
Charles Petzold • ISBN 0-7356-2153-5

CLR via C++
Jeffrey Richter with Stanley B. Lippman
ISBN 0-7356-2248-5

Programming Microsoft Web Forms
Douglas J. Reilly • ISBN 0-7356-2179-9

Debugging, Tuning, and Testing Microsoft .NET 2.0 Applications
John Robbins • ISBN 0-7356-2202-7

For more information about Microsoft Press® books and other learning products,
visit: **www.microsoft.com/books** *and* **www.microsoft.com/learning**

Additional Resources for Visual Basic Developers

Published and Forthcoming Titles from Microsoft Press

Microsoft® Visual Basic® 2005 Express Edition: Build a Program Now!
Patrice Pelland • ISBN 0-7356-2213-2

Featuring a full working edition of the software, this fun and highly visual guide walks you through a complete programming project—a desktop weather-reporting application—from start to finish. You'll get an introduction to the Microsoft Visual Studio® development environment and learn how to put the lightweight, easy-to-use tools in Visual Basic Express to work right away—creating, compiling, testing, and delivering your first ready-to-use program. You'll get expert tips, coaching, and visual examples each step of the way, along with pointers to additional learning resources.

Microsoft Visual Basic 2005 *Step by Step*
Michael Halvorson • ISBN 0-7356-2131-4

With enhancements across its visual designers, code editor, language, and debugger that help accelerate the development and deployment of robust, elegant applications across the Web, a business group, or an enterprise, Visual Basic 2005 focuses on enabling developers to rapidly build applications. Now you can teach yourself the essentials of working with Visual Studio 2005 and the new features of the Visual Basic language—one step at a time. Each chapter puts you to work, showing you how, when, and why to use specific features of Visual Basic and guiding as you create actual components and working applications for Microsoft Windows®. You'll also explore data management and Web-based development topics.

Programming Microsoft Visual Basic 2005 *Core Reference*
Francesco Balena • ISBN 0-7356-2183-7

Get the expert insights, indispensable reference, and practical instruction needed to exploit the core language features and capabilities in Visual Basic 2005. Well-known Visual Basic programming author Francesco Balena expertly guides you through the fundamentals, including modules, keywords, and inheritance, and builds your mastery of more advanced topics such as delegates, assemblies, and My Namespace. Combining in-depth reference with extensive, hands-on code examples and best-practices advice, this *Core Reference* delivers the key resources that you need to develop professional-level programming skills for smart clients and the Web.

Programming Microsoft Visual Basic 2005 Framework Reference
Francesco Balena • ISBN 0-7356-2175-6

Complementing *Programming Microsoft Visual Basic 2005 Core Reference*, this book covers a wide range of additional topics and information critical to Visual Basic developers, including Windows Forms, working with Microsoft ADO.NET 2.0 and ASP.NET 2.0, Web services, security, remoting, and much more. Packed with sample code and real-world examples, this book will help developers move from understanding to mastery.

Programming Microsoft Windows Forms
Charles Petzold • ISBN 0-7356-2153-5

Programming Microsoft Web Forms
Douglas J. Reilly • ISBN 0-7356-2179-9

Debugging, Tuning, and Testing Microsoft .NET 2.0 Applications
John Robbins • ISBN 0-7356-2202-7

Microsoft ASP.NET 2.0 *Step by Step*
George Shepherd • ISBN 0-7356-2201-9

Microsoft ADO.NET 2.0 *Step by Step*
Rebecca Riordan • ISBN 0-7356-2164-0

Programming Microsoft ASP.NET 2.0 *Core Reference*
Dino Esposito • ISBN 0-7356-2176-4

For more information about Microsoft Press® books and other learning products, visit: **www.microsoft.com/books** *and* **www.microsoft.com/learning**

What do you think of this book?

We want to hear from you!

Do you have a few minutes to participate in a brief online survey?

Microsoft is interested in hearing your feedback so we can continually improve our books and learning resources for you.

To participate in our survey, please visit:

www.microsoft.com/learning/booksurvey/

...and enter this book's ISBN-10 number (appears above barcode on back cover*).
As a thank-you to survey participants in the United States and Canada, each month we'll randomly select five respondents to win one of five $100 gift certificates from a leading online merchant. At the conclusion of the survey, you can enter the drawing by providing your e-mail address, which will be used for prize notification only.

Thanks in advance for your input. Your opinion counts!

* Where to find the ISBN-10 on back cover

ISBN-13: 000-0-0000-0000-0
ISBN-10: 0-0000-0000-0

Example only. Each book has unique ISBN.

***Microsoft*® Press**